T0328487

Statistics, Econometrics and Forecasting

Based on two lectures presented as part of the Stone Lectures in Economics series, Arnold Zellner describes the structural econometric time series analysis (SEMTSA) approach to statistical and econometric modeling. Developed by Zellner and Franz Palm, the SEMTSA approach produces an understanding of the relationship of univariate and multivariate time series forecasting models and dynamic time series structural econometric models. As scientists and decision-makers in industry and government worldwide adopt the Bayesian approach to scientific inference, decision-making and forecasting, Zellner offers an in-depth analysis and appreciation of this important paradigm shift. Finally, Zellner discusses the alternative approaches to model building and looks at how the use and development of the SEMTSA approach has led to the production of a Marshallian macroeconomic model that will prove valuable to many. Written by one of the foremost practitioners of econometrics, this book will have wide academic and professional appeal.

ARNOLD ZELLNER is H. G. B. Alexander Distinguished Service Professor Emeritus of Economics and Statistics at the University of Chicago, and Adjunct Professor at the University of California at Berkeley. He is one of the most important figures in the development of econometrics, in particular the use of Bayesian techniques. Professor Zellner was President of the American Statistical Association in 1991, and the first-elected President of the International Society for Bayesian Analysis in 1993. He is an elected Fellow of leading professional organizations. He is co-founder of the *Journal of Econometrics*, and remains an active researcher in modeling, statistics and forecasting.

National Institute of Economic and Social Research

The National Institute of Economic and Social Research is an independent educational charity, founded in 1938. It conducts research on a wide variety of topics, but has a particular interest in economic modelling, investment and productivity, labour market issues and vocational education and training. All research projects are designed to contribute to the public debate on the issues they address. The Institute has its own research staff based in central London, and works in co-operation with universities, industry and other bodies. It is independent of the UK government and receives no core funding from public or private sources.

The Institute aims to promote, through quantitative research, a deeper understanding of the interaction of economic and social forces that affect people's lives, in order that they may be improved. Its main function is to produce research suitable for publication through academic channels, and hence findings from the Institute's work are published widely in academic journals and elsewhere. They often find an outlet in the Institute's own quarterly *Economic Review* which is available on subscription or individually. Discussion Papers dealing with work in progress, and Occasional Papers on specific topics, are also issued from time to time. Results from major pieces of research often lead to books, published through commercial publishers. In addition, the NIESR holds conferences each year, which provide an opportunity to hear about research findings and debate them with interested organisations and individuals.

National Institute of Economic and Social Research
2 Dean Trench Street, London SW1P 3HE
Tel: 020 7654 1920   Fax: 020 7654 1900

The Bank of England Centre for Central Banking Studies

The Bank of England's Centre for Central Banking Studies was founded in 1991. Its main aims then were twofold. First, to provide training for staff in the central banks of countries emerging from many decades of communist government; and second, to create a formal mechanism for enhancing training contact and advice with and for the forty-five or so (mainly Commonwealth) central banks in the old sterling area with which the Bank of England had long-standing links. Since then, the CCBS has widened its range of contacts and activities considerably. It has now accumulated a stock of over ten thousand alumni. Over 120 of the world's central banks, some occasionally and others on a large and regular basis, are now involved in its seminars, courses, technical assistance programmes, conferences and research workshops and projects each year. Many of these take place in London. There is also a growing number of CCBS events overseas, many embracing several countries in the region, run in collaboration with foreign central banks or multi-country institutions. In all it does, the CCBS emphasises the importance of learning from the diverse experiences of all countries, and providing a forum where ideas and experiences are shared.

Subjects range from traditional central bank concerns such as note issue, monetary operations, reserves management, payments systems, human resources, and accounting and audit, to econometrics, forecasting for monetary policy, exchange rates, capital movements, inflation, financial markets, derivatives, policy communication, financial stability and corporate governance.

Econometrics now plays a vital role in helping to inform monetary policy makers about key relationships in their economy, and to improve and sharpen predictions (and pinpoint areas of uncertainty) about the likely consequences, over time, of the policy decisions they take. Speakers at CCBS functions are drawn from experts in the CCBS itself, other parts of the Bank of England, other central banks, the UK private sector, and the academic community, both in Britain and abroad. An increasing number of the CCBS conferences – devoted to economic and econometric issues – are now open to, and attended by, academics and practitioners outside central banks.

Richard Stone was a highly creative and prolific econometrician and applied economist; he left his distinguished mark in countless areas of the subject, and not least on those techniques and concepts encountered, debated and deployed daily by professional economists in the world's central banks. The CCBS (and, indeed, the Bank of England more generally) were delighted to accept the invitation to participate with Cambridge University Press and the National Institute of Economic and Social Research in helping to host the Stone Lectures. These are a very fitting monument to Sir Richard's achievements, and correspond closely to the CCBS's objective of sharing and helping to disseminate the best of important new thinking on financial, economic and, above all, econometric issues to the world-wide community – and, thereby, contribute to a better understanding of how to preserve and enhance monetary and financial stability.

Peter Sinclair
Director of the CCBS, 2000–2002, and Professor of Economics, University of Birmingham

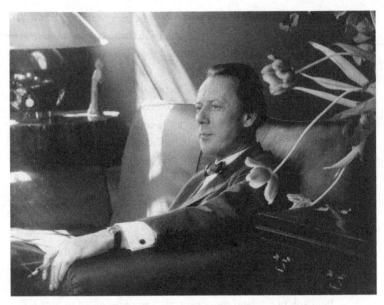

Sir Richard Stone, Nobel Laureate in Economics

THE STONE LECTURES IN ECONOMICS

Statistics, Econometrics and Forecasting

Arnold Zellner

University of Chicago

CAMBRIDGE
UNIVERSITY PRESS

CAMBRIDGE UNIVERSITY PRESS
Cambridge, New York, Melbourne, Madrid, Cape Town, Singapore, São Paulo

Cambridge University Press
The Edinburgh Building, Cambridge CB2 8RU, UK

Published in the United States of America by Cambridge University Press, New York

www.cambridge.org
Information on this title: www.cambridge.org/9780521832878

First published 2004

A catalogue record for this publication is available from the British Library

ISBN 978-0-521-83287-8 hardback
ISBN 978-0-521-54044-5 paperback

Transferred to digital printing 2008

Contents

Figures

Tables

Preface

It was indeed a great honor and pleasure to present the first Sir Richard Stone Lectures in London in May 2001. My thanks go to the National Institute for Economic and Social Research (NIESR) and the Cambridge University Press (CUP) for instituting the Stone Lectures and inviting me to be the first speaker in this series. I appreciate very much the opportunity to express my thoughts on the outstanding contributions of Sir Richard Stone and on statistics, econometrics and forecasting.

As explained to me by Martin Weale, director of the NIESR, and my editor at CUP, the first 2001 Stone Lecture was to be presented at the Bank of England with many "non-technical" attendees in the audience. Thus, in the first Lecture I decided to treat some broad, basic issues involved in Stone's, and others', work in statistics, econometrics and forecasting, since these are important for both non-technical and technical individuals and often are not well treated in standard textbooks. Indeed, it may be advisable to consider introducing good courses in the philosophy of science in the curricula of departments and schools of statistics, economics and econometrics, as is already the case in the programs of some departments of physics and other sciences. Issues such as (1) "What is science?" (2) "What is causality?" and (3) "What definition of probability is most useful in scientific work?" can be considered, along with many others, and thereby help to eliminate confusion that sometimes lasts a lifetime. And, of course, such courses can educate students to do productive, innovative research rather than humdrum, conventional or – worse – pointless research. In this connection, close study of Stone's approach to research and the results yielded by it, which had a profound impact on many research efforts, including my own, from my doctoral dissertation research onward, would be most fruitful.

Another important topic treated in my first lecture is a basic paradigm shift that is taking place in statistics, econometrics and forecasting. About 200 years after Thomas Bayes, a British Presbyterian minister and Fellow of the Royal Society, introduced Bayes' Theorem in a 1763 paper, it appears that scientists and decision-makers in industry and government worldwide are adopting the Bayesian approach to scientific inference, decision-making and forecasting, as developed over the years by Laplace, Edgeworth, Jeffreys, de Finetti, Savage, Good, Box and many others. For appreciation of this paradigm shift in the non-technical literature, see, e.g., "Banks tap ideas from 18th-century minister" in the *International Herald Tribune*, August 21–22, 1999, and "In praise of Bayes" in *The Economist*, September 30, 2000, for some current thoughts about and applications of Bayesian analysis. For additional evidence, see material in J. Berger's and others' papers in the December 2000 issue of the *Journal of the American Statistical Association* on a review of the current state of Bayesian analysis and computing in Statistics and related fields, and material on the homepage of the International Society for Bayesian Analysis (ISBA) website (http://www.Bayesian.org). Further, a number of explicit, basic Bayes / non-Bayes issues are discussed in detail in my lecture, with the conclusion that "It pays to go Bayes."

Finally, some simple examples are included in the first lecture to demonstrate operational aspects of the general principles and procedures. That simple, intuitive solutions to central problems, including some educational management problems as well as golf club selection problems, are available may come as a surprise to many. Indeed, given that higher education is managed by many who have never taken courses in management, i.e. personnel management, financial management, inventory management, etc., it may be that some of these examples can serve as subject matter for such courses and possibly help to improve the performance of higher education.

In the second lecture, presented at the NIESR, I was advised that the audience would be more academic and technically sophisticated. Thus, I go into more mathematical detail in describing the structural econometric, time series analysis approach to statistical and econometric modeling that Franz Palm and I developed, which has been applied to a variety of problems over the years by us and many colleagues. A CUP volume on SEMTSA and its applications, edited by Franz Palm and me, has been prepared for publication.

The SEMTSA approach produces an understanding of the relationship between univariate and multivariate time series forecasting models and dynamic, time series structural econometric models. For many years, this relationship was not understood and the situation appeared somewhat confused. Some believed that univariate statistical time series forecasting models, e.g. Box-Jenkins' autoregressive, integrated moving average (ARIMA) and transfer function models, and multivariate econometric structural models were distinct and seemingly unrelated. As shown in the second lecture, these models are closely related, and use of the relationships involves very important procedures for model formulation and checking that have been applied over the years. That is, when there is little information about the form of a structural econometric model, in the SEMTSA approach, univariate dynamic forecasting equations for individual variables are developed and checked in forecasting – not only point forecasting but also turning point forecasting studies. When equations are found that perform satisfactorily in forecasting, work is then undertaken to formulate a dynamic multi-equation economic model that implies the forms of the individual variables' univariate forecasting equations. Then the multivariate time series structural model can be implemented and its properties and forecasting performance evaluated.

And, of course, given a current statistical or econometric multivariate time series model – say, a vector autoregression (VAR) or a dynamic structural macroeconometric model – in the SEMTSA approach the univariate processes for individual variables are derived analytically from the general model and their forms, e.g. lag structures etc., are checked using data. Many times, as shown in empirical studies, such derived relations for individual variables, which are often very complicated, are at variance with the forms of equations empirically derived from data. Recognition of such discrepancies between theoretically implied equations and empirically determined equations often leads to improvements in theoretical formulations and forecasting performance.

Some examples of such work are provided in the second lecture in connection with work to forecast the output growth rates of industrialized countries and turning points in them. Bayesian point, turning point and forecast combining techniques, which have been developed and applied with some success, are described. In addition, the sequential SEMTSA approach has led to the consideration of disaggregation and forecasting performance, a topic not extensively treated in the literature. The results of some forecasting experiments involving disaggregation and of work to formulate a disaggregated model of an economy, namely a Marshallian macroeconomic model (MMM), are described. The MMM involves modeling sectors of economies using relatively simple Marshallian sector demand, supply and entry equations to model interacting sectors of an economy – say, agriculture, mining, services, etc. The results of some recent forecasting experiments using data for the U.S. economy indicates that it pays to disaggregate in this case when using the MMM.

Throughout the two lectures there is an emphasis on the value of "sophisticatedly simple" models, in contrast to the grossly complicated models of economies that many have built in the past. Some of these past models have hundreds of non-linear stochastic difference equations and variables and thus it is difficult to determine whether they have unique or multiple solutions and what their dynamic properties are. Further, these complicated models have not been very successful in point and turning point forecasting. Thus, as recognized by workers worldwide, including researchers at the Bank of England (see, e.g., the article by Paul Fisher and John Whitley, "Macroeconomic models at the Bank of England," in the 2000 volume edited by Sean Holly and Martin Weale, *Econometric Modelling: Techniques and Applications*), there is a great need for sophisticatedly simple models that explain the past well and perform satisfactorily in forecasting and helping to make policy decisions. In a recent CUP monograph, *Simplicity, Inference and Modeling*, edited by H. A. Kuezenkamp, M. McAleer and me, many issues, including defining and measuring the simplicity of models and simplicity versus complexity in modeling, are discussed extensively by leading workers. Keeping it sophisticatedly simple (KISS) seems to be appreciated and valued by many, including economists awarded Nobel Prizes, whose responses to a survey on simplicity versus complexity are summarized in the above monograph.

Again, I thank the sponsors of the Sir Richard Stone Lectures for giving me an opportunity to share my ideas with you. Thanks also go to Martin Weale and to the staff of CUP for arranging my wife's and my enjoyable visits to Cambridge, London and York and for a splendid dinner in my honor, at which I met Sir Richard Stone's charming wife and learned much from our discussions. In all respects it was a wonderful experience, memories of which we shall treasure always. Last, but not least, thanks to Barbara Birthwright, my secretary, for her valuable assistance in preparing this manuscript for publication.

1

Bank of England

MAY 8, 2001

1.1 Introduction

There can be no doubt but that Sir Richard Stone is a true economic scientist, one of those who contributed importantly to the transition of economics from being an art to being a science. Significantly, he emphasized and practiced "measurement with theory," not "measurement without theory" nor "theory without measurement." In doing so, he set an excellent example for many others who followed his lead. His careful and thorough measurement procedures and use of sophisticatedly simple theoretical economic models and impressive statistical techniques in analyses of important problems brought him worldwide recognition, as recognized by many, including Angus Deaton[1] in the following words:

> Sir Richard Stone, knighted in 1978, and Nobel Laureate in Economics in 1984, is the outstanding figure in post-war British applied economics . . . Under Keynes' stimulus, the Cambridge Department of Applied Economics was founded and Richard Stone was appointed its first director with an indefinite tenure in the position. Stone brought enormous distinction and worldwide recognition to the department . . . He was president of the Econometric Society in 1955 and president of the Royal Economic Society from 1978–90.

Further, in an article, "The life and work of John Richard Nicholas Stone 1913–1991," that appeared in the *Economic Journal*, M. H. Pesaran and G. C. Harcourt (2000, p. 146) wrote:

> Sir Richard Stone . . . was one of the pioneers of national income and social accounts, and one of the few economists of his generation to have faced the challenge of economics as a science by combining theory and measurement within a cohesive framework. Awarded the Nobel Prize for his 'fundamental contributions to the development of national accounts', he made equally significant contributions to the empirical analysis of consumer behaviour. His work on the 'Growth Project' was instrumental in the development of econometric methodology for the construction and analysis of large disaggregated macroeconometric models.

Also, they presented the following excerpt from Stone's research proposal for the now famous Department of Applied Economics at Cambridge with Stone as its first director in 1945 (pp. 149–150):

> The ultimate aim of applied economics is to increase human welfare by the investigation and analysis of economic problems of the real world. It is the view of the Department that this can best be achieved by the synthesis of three types of study which now tend to be pursued in isolation. The Department will concentrate simultaneously on the work of observations, i.e. the discovery and preparation of data; the theoretical appraisal of problems, i.e. the framing of hypotheses in a form suitable for quantitative testing; and the development of statistical methods appropriate to the special problems of economic information. The special character of the Department's approach to problems of the real world will lie in this attempt at systematic synthesis.

From what has been presented above, it is clear that Stone had a deep appreciation of methodological issues and an approach that was very productive. Note that Pearson, Jeffreys, Fisher, I^2 and many others are in broad agreement with Stone's position and have emphasized the "unity of science" principle, namely that any area of study (e.g., economics, physics, business, psychology, sports, etc.) can be a science if scientific methods are employed in learning from data and experience to explain the past, predict and make wise decisions – fundamental objectives of science. To achieve these objectives, scientists use methods that will now briefly be reviewed.

It has been recognized that scientists generally employ the process of induction, which involves (a) measurement and description and (b) use of generalizations or theories to explain, predict and make decisions. This view of induction is much broader than that of Mach's, which involves equating induction to empirical measurement. In doing so, Mach missed the very important activities of explanation, prediction and decision-making that are involved in the above, broader definition of induction. Similarly, attempts by others to equate science, particularly economic science, to deduction is a fundamental mistake since in deduction just limiting statements of proof, disproof or ignorance are possible. Scientists need and use statements reflecting degrees of confidence in propositions or generalizations that cannot be analyzed using only deductive methods. For example, it is impossible to prove deductively that the sun will rise tomorrow. This point is very important with respect to those who, in contrast to Stone and many others, hold the view that economics is a purely deductive science. Deduction, including mathematical proof, plays a role but the broader process of induction is needed in science. Later I shall discuss how probabilities to represent degrees of confidence in propositions or theories can be utilized in the process of learning from data and making decisions. Finally, there is the area of "reduction," in which work is undertaken to produce generalizations or theories that explain the past, predict well and are useful in making decisions; this will be discussed below.

A key element in the inductive process is measurement and description, as Stone, Jeffreys, Fisher and others have recognized. As widely appreciated, it is important to measure well important variables such as unemployment, output, prices, income, saving, etc. for a variety of purposes. Fortunately, much progress over the years has been made in improving the quality of measurements, e.g. quality-corrected price indices, consistent national income and product accounts, etc. However, many other improvements can be made, e.g. in the measurement of the output of government and education sectors and of personal saving. Such measurements are important inputs to those who study economies' past performance and attempt to forecast future outcomes – that is, professional and amateur forecasters. Also, these measurements are important inputs to those engaged in the process of "reduction" – that is, creation of theories to explain past data and help to predict as yet unobserved data. For example, the famous Kuznets research finding that the US savings rate was relatively constant over the first half of the twentieth century in spite of huge increases in real income was a surprising empirical result, in sharp contradiction to the Keynesian prediction that the savings rate would rise.[3] Several, including Friedman, Modigliani, Tobin and others, created new theories to explain the surprising empirically observed constancy of the savings rate. Further, as Hadamard[4] reported in his study of creative work in mathematics, new breakthroughs in mathematics and other fields are often produced after observing "unusual facts." In view of this connection between productive reductive activity and unusual facts, in past work I have described[5] a number of ways to produce unusual facts: e.g., study unusual historical periods – say, periods of hyperinflation or great depression; study unusual groups, e.g. very poor producers and consumers; push current theories to extremes and empirically check their predictions, etc. Also, my advice to empirical workers in economics is: produce unusual facts that need explanation and ugly facts (which Thomas Huxley emphasized as being important, namely facts that sharply contradict current theories), instead of humdrum, boring facts.

Above, I mentioned that forecasters are vitally interested in inductive measurement problems and require good data with which to develop effective statistical forecasting procedures and models. For many years, forecasting models, e.g. the univariate autoregressive moving average (ARMA) forecasting models of Box and Jenkins and the multivariate ARMA models of Quenouille,[6] which include a vector autoregressive (VAR) model as a special case, were considered to be distinct from the structural econometric models (SEMs) constructed by economists such as Tinbergen, Klein, Stone and many others. In a 1974 paper,[7] Palm and I not only demonstrated the relationship between univariate and multivariate ARMA models and structural econometric models but also illustrated how that relationship can be exploited to produce improved SEMs in the structural econometric, time series analysis approach. This combination of forecasting and structural modeling approaches has been very fruitful and will be illustrated below.

In addition, I, along with many others, have emphasized the importance of sophisticated simplicity in modeling. Note that, in industry, there is the expression KISS: that is, "Keep It Simple, Stupid." Since some simple models are stupid, I decided to reinterpret KISS to mean: "Keep It Sophisticatedly Simple." Indeed, there are many sophisticatedly simple models that work reasonably well in many sciences, e.g. $s = 1/2gt^2$, $F = ma$, $PV = RT$, $E = mc^2$, the laws of demand and supply, etc. Over the years I have challenged many audiences to tell me about one complicated model that works well in explanation and prediction and have not heard of a single one. Certainly, large-scale econometric models, VARs and other complex models have not worked very well in explanation and prediction in economics. For evidence on these points, see, e.g., McNees, Zarnowitz, Fair, and Fisher and Whitley.[8]

Further, after years of application, the "general to specific" approach that involves starting with a complicated large model, often a linear VAR, and testing downward to obtain a good model has not as yet been successful. There are many, many general models and if one chooses the wrong one, as is usually the case, results are doomed to be unsatisfactory. Starting simply and complicating if necessary is an approach that has worked well in many sciences and is favored by Jeffreys, Friedman, Tobin and many others. For further consideration of these issues of simplicity versus complexity and methods of measuring the simplicity of economic models, see the papers in the recent Cambridge University Press monograph, *Simplicity, Inference and Modeling*.[9]

With this said about some key philosophical issues involved in statistics, econometrics and forecasting, we now come to the fundamental Bayes/non-Bayes statistical/econometric methodological controversies that have been raging since the publication of Bayes' 1763 paper.[10] These controversies are focused on the issues of (1) how to learn from data effectively, (2) how to estimate effects and test for their presence or absence, (3) how to use data to make good forecasts and decisions, and (4) how to produce models or laws that work well in explanation, prediction and decision-making. Many leading workers worldwide, including Laplace, Edgeworth, Jeffreys, Fisher, Neyman, Pearson, de Finetti, Savage, Box, Lindley, Good and many others, have been involved in these controversies, which are still ongoing. What is at issue in such debates and discussions is, fundamentally: "how do we operationally perform scientific inference – that is, induction and reduction – that involves effective learning from data, making wise decisions, and producing good models or laws that are helpful in explanation, prediction and decision-making?" It is my view that the Bayesian approach is emerging as the principal paradigm for use in science and decision-making. For recent information on the explosive upward movement in the volume of Bayesian publications with many references, some to free downloadable Bayesian computer software, including the University of Cambridge's famous "BUGS" program, see Berger's December 2000 *Journal of the American Statistical Association* article and material and references on the homepages of the International Society for Bayesian Analysis website, http://www.Bayesian.org, and of the Section on Bayesian Statistical Science (SBSS) of the American Statistical Association (ASA) website, http://www.amstat.org. Also, the annual SBSS/ISBA proceedings volumes contain many valuable articles in which Bayesian methods are developed and applied to forecasting, financial portfolio and other problems. Then, too, the recent proceedings volume for the ISBA 2000 world meeting, which was published in 2001 by Eurostat (the statistical office of the European Communities),[11] includes Bayesian papers dealing with many basic theoretical and applied problems.

1.2 Overview of the Bayesian approach

Basic to the Bayesian approach is the Bayesian learning model, Bayes' theorem, which has been applied successfully to a wide range of problems encountered in statistics, econometrics, forecasting and other areas. Generally we utilize the Bayesian model to learn about values of parameters – say, appearing in forecasting or demand equations – as follows: in step 1, our initial or "prior" information, denoted by I, regarding possible values of the parameters in the vector $\theta' = (\theta_1, \theta_2, \ldots, \theta_m)$ is summarized in a prior probability density function, denoted by $\pi(\theta \mid I)$. In step 2, we represent the information in our current data, y, by use of a likelihood function, denoted by $L(\theta \mid y, I)$. In step 3, we combine our prior information and our sample information, using Bayes' theorem, to obtain a posterior distribution for the parameters, as follows:

$$g(\theta \mid y, I) = c\pi(\theta \mid I)L(\theta \mid y, I) \tag{1.1}$$

where c, the factor of proportionality, is a normalizing constant such that $\int g(\theta \mid y, I) \, d\theta = 1$. It is the case that g in equation (1.1) contains all the information, prior and sample, and thus (1.1) is a 100 percent efficient information processing procedure, as I have shown in the recent literature[12] regarding a new information theoretic derivation of (1.1). What was done was to consider the problem as an engineer might do, namely to consider measures of the input information and of the output information and to find a proper output density, g, that minimizes the difference between the output information and the input information. Using conventional information measures, surprisingly, the solution to this problem is given in equation (1.1), Bayes' theorem. See discussion of this result by Jaynes, Hill, Kullback, Bernardo and Smith after my first paper on this topic.[13] In particular, Jaynes remarked that this demonstration was the first to show a direct connection between information theory (or entropy theory) and Bayes' theorem, and that there was much more work that could be done to produce other, perhaps more general, learning rules. In my response to Jaynes and others, and in my later work, some such extensions have been derived to provide a variety of static and dynamic learning models, which are generalized versions of Bayes' theorem reflecting additional conditions and constraints.

In addition to the above information theoretic derivation of Bayes' theorem, a traditional probability theory proof of Bayes' theorem is available to justify (1.1). That is, from the joint probability density function (pdf), $p(y, \theta)$ for the observations, y, and the parameter vector, θ, we have, given our prior information I, $p(\theta, y \mid I) = \pi(\theta \mid I) f(y \mid \theta, I) = h(y \mid I) g(\theta \mid y, I)$ from the product rule of probability, where $f(y \mid \theta, I)$ is the pdf for the observations given the parameters and prior information and $h(y \mid I)$ is the marginal density of the observations. Then on solving for $g(\theta \mid y, I)$, we have:

$$g(\theta \mid y, I) = \pi(\theta \mid I) L(\theta \mid y, I) / h(y \mid I) \qquad (1.2)$$

with the likelihood function defined by $L(\theta \mid y, I) \equiv f(y \mid \theta, I)$ and $1/h(y \mid I)$ is the factor of proportionality c in equation (1.1). Note that the derivation of (1.2) via probability theory relies on the product rule of probability; see Jeffreys[14] for a penetrating discussion of the assumptions needed for proof of the product rule of probability, which he points out may not be satisfied in all circumstances, and his admission that he was not able to derive an alternative proof under weaker conditions, which led him to introduce the product rule not as a theorem but as an axiom in his theory of probability. Thus it is interesting to note, as pointed out above, that Bayes' theorem or learn-ing model, and generalizations of it, can also be derived as solutions to optimization problems.

Having the posterior density in (1.2), it is well known that it can be employed to calculate the probability that a parameter's value lies between a and b, two given numbers, and to construct poste-rior confidence intervals and regions for a parameter or set of pa-rameters. Also, an optimal estimate for parameters is obtained by choosing such an estimate to minimize the posterior expectation of a given loss function. For example, for a quadratic loss function, it is well known that the optimal estimate for θ is the posterior mean, $\theta^* = E\theta \mid D = \int \theta g(\theta \mid D) \, d\theta$, where $D = (y, I)$; for an absolute error loss function, it is the median; and, for a zero-one loss function, it is the modal value. Optimal estimates have been derived for many other loss functions, including "two-part" loss functions,[15] e.g. with one part emphasizing goodness of fit, as in least squares, and the other precision of estimation. It has also been recognized in many problems, including medical, real estate assessment, policy and forecasting, that asymmetry of loss functions is of great practical importance. For example, in fore-casting it is often the case that over-forecasting by a certain amount can be much more serious than an under-forecast of the same magnitude. The same is true in the medical area. There are now many papers in the literature dealing with the solution of problems involving asymmetric loss functions.[16] That estimates and predictions that are optimal rel-ative to asymmetric loss functions can be easily computed and often differ substantially from those that are optimal relative to symmet-ric loss functions is most noteworthy. In non-Bayesian approaches to inference, it is not as direct to derive estimates, predictions and forecasts that are optimal relative to asymmetric and many other loss functions.

Further, analytically and empirically, it has been established that op-timal Bayesian estimates have rather good sampling properties – that is, good average performance in repeated trials, as when a procedure is built into a computer program and used over and over again on similar problems. Of course, if we are concerned about just one decision, the criterion of performance in repeated samples may not be very relevant, just as in visiting a restaurant on a particular evening. Many times we are just concerned with the performance of the restaurant on one evening, not on average. However, in some contexts average performance – say, in ranking restaurants, or wines, or statistical procedures – is relevant, and it is fortunate that Bayesian procedures have good average performance or risk properties, as shown analytically and in Monte Carlo experiments. For some recent striking examples of the outstanding performance of Bayesian estimators vis-à-vis non-Bayesian estimators in the case of estimating the parameters of the widely used Nerlove agricultural supply model, see papers by Diebold and Lamb, and Shen and Perloff, and – for other models – Tsurumi, Park, Gao and Lahiri, and Zellner.[17] In these studies, the sampling performance of various Bayesian estimation procedures was shown to be better than that of leading non-Bayesian estimation procedures, including maximum likelihood, Fuller's modified maximum likelihood, two-stage least squares, ordinary least squares, etc.

Further, Bayesian methods have been utilized to produce Stein-like shrinkage estimates and forecasts that have rather good sampling and forecasting properties; see, e.g., Berger, Jorion, Min and Zellner, Quintana, Putnam and their colleagues, Zellner, Hong and Min, Zellner and Vandaele[18] and references cited in these works. Quintana and Putnam talk about "shrinking forecasts to stretch returns" in connection with their work in forecasting returns to form financial portfolios using Bayesian optimization procedures. It is indeed the case that improved estimation and forecasting techniques are not only of theoretical interest but are having an impact on practical applications in financial portfolio formation, forecasting and other areas.

Now, suppose that we partition the vector of parameters in the posterior density in equation (1.2) as follows, $\theta = (\theta_1, \theta_2)$, and that we are interested in learning about the value of θ_1 and regard the parameters in θ_2 to be "nuisance" parameters. How do we get rid of the nuisance parameters? The answer is very simple; we just integrate them out of the joint posterior density – a standard procedure in the calculus that can be performed analytically or numerically. That is, the marginal density for θ_1 is simply given by integrating θ_2 out of the joint density to obtain the marginal density for θ_1 as follows:

$$g(\theta_1 \mid D) = \int g(\theta_1, \theta_2 \mid D) \, d\theta_2$$

$$= \int g(\theta_1|\theta_2, D)g(\theta_2 \mid D) \, d\theta_2 \qquad (1.3)$$

where, in the second line of (1.3), $g(\theta_1 \mid \theta_2, D)$ is the conditional density for θ_1 given θ_2 and the data, D, and $g(\theta_2 \mid D)$ is the marginal density of θ_2 given the data.

Thus integration, analytical or numerical, as shown in (1.3), is a very useful way to get rid of nuisance parameters. Note, from the second line of (1.3), the integration can be viewed as an averaging of conditional densities for θ_1 given θ_2 to obtain the marginal density. This is quite different from substituting an estimate of θ_2 in the conditional density $g(\theta_1 \mid \theta_2, D)$ in an effort to deal with the nuisance parameter problem. Such a "solution" has often been found to be a poor one in small sample situations. Also, the conditional posterior density can provide much information regarding the sensitivity of inferences about θ_1 to values assigned to θ_2. For illustrations of such uses of conditional posterior densities, see, e.g., books by Box and Tiao, Poirier, Zellner and others.[19]

Thus, in contrast to difficulties in the treatment of nuisance parameters experienced in other approaches to statistics and econometrics, it is straightforward to get rid of nuisance parameters in the Bayesian approach: just integrate them out of the joint density and use the marginal density to make inferences about parameters of interest, e.g. to compute a mean of the marginal density as an optimal point estimate vis-à-vis a quadratic loss function or to compute posterior intervals or regions for parameters of interest. Further, from the second line of equation (1.3), as noted above, it has been recognized in the literature that the integration can be viewed mathematically as an averaging of the conditional densities for θ_1 given θ_2 with the marginal density for θ_2 used as the weight function. Also, the conditional density, $g(\theta_1 \mid \theta_2, D)$, has been employed in many investigations to determine how sensitive inferences about parameters of interest are to what is assumed about the values of the nuisance parameters. That is, posterior densities and moments of parameters of interest can be computed from the conditional density for various assumed values of nuisance parameters to study the nature of the dependence of results on what is assumed about the values of nuisance parameters. And, of course, Bayesian posterior odds (to be discussed below) can be employed to investigate various hypotheses regarding the alternative values of the nuisance parameters, e.g. that an autocorrelation parameter is equal to zero, versus the hypotheses that it has a negative or a positive value.

In summary, we have an operational learning model given in (1.1) that has been derived in various ways and applied successfully in solving many problems. To provide illustrative specific analyses of some concrete problems, suppose our data are five observed heads in five tosses of a coin. What can we say about the probability of a head appearing on the next flip? Generally, if we assume that the coin is fair and tossed fairly and thus the probability on any toss, including the next, is 1/2, this is a problem in "direct" probability; that is, we know the probability and, given this information, predict the outcomes. However, when we don't have this information regarding whether the coin is fair and tossed fairly we cannot safely assume that the probability is 1/2 but, rather, have to use the information in the outcomes or data – five heads in five tosses – to infer or guess the value of this probability, which can range from zero to one, and this is a problem in what is usually referred to as "inverse inference." That is, we go from the information in the data back to infer or guess the value of θ, in contrast to a problem in "direct" probability, where we assume a known value of θ and use it to predict outcomes.

Let $\theta =$ the value of the probability of a head on a single fair toss that has an unknown value in the interval zero to one (note that the information that a head has appeared is information that the probability is not exactly equal to zero; the case of a "two-tailed" coin). Also, we shall assume that θ is constant from trial to trial and that the trials are independent. With these assumptions, the probability of observing five heads in five independent trials – the data – is just θ^5, the product of the probabilities for the five independent events, which is the likelihood function for this problem. Further suppose that we have little information about the value of θ and follow Laplace and others by representing our "diffuse" or "ignorance" prior by a uniform prior[20] – that is, $\pi(\theta) = 1$ for $0 < 0 < 1$. Then our posterior density is: $g(\theta \mid D) = c\pi(\theta)L(\theta \mid D) = 6\theta^5$, where $c = 6$ is the normalizing constant and the density has a mode or highest value at $\theta = 1$, an optimal estimate vis-à-vis a "zero-one" loss function[21] and mean $E\theta = 6/7$, an optimal point estimate relative to the squared error loss function, $L(\theta, \hat{\theta}) = (\theta - \hat{\theta})^2$, and a special case of Laplace's "rule of succession," namely that $(n + 1)/(n + 2) =$ the posterior mean, given n heads in n trials.

Having the complete, exact posterior density for θ permits us not only to obtain optimal point estimates relative to various loss functions but also to compute the probability that θ lies between any two values – say, a and b, the original problem posed by Bayes. For example, $\Pr(0.5 < \theta < 1 \mid D) = 6\int_{1/2}^{1} \theta^5 \, d\theta = 1 - 1/64 = 63/64$, a rather high value. Also, if we use the posterior mean $= 6/7$ as our estimate, the probability of a head appearing on the next toss is $6/7$ – quite different from $1/2$, the value associated with a fairly tossed, fair coin. These and many other valuable probability statements can be made, based on the given prior density and the information in the likelihood function.[22]

A similar set-up can be employed in connection with five independent tests of the validity of a theory, with θ being the probability that the theory is valid, or in connection with five male births in five trials, as is the case with my wife and me, with θ being the probability of a male birth on a given trial, and ask: "What is the probability that the next birth will be a male child?" Using the above results, the expected value of θ, 6/7, is a best estimate relative to a quadratic loss function, given the prior and sample information described above. On the other hand, if our loss function is a "zero-one" loss function, our optimal point estimate is the modal value of the posterior density, which in this case is one.

We treated the above two problems as pure estimation problems. If we want to consider alternative assumptions – say, hypothesis 1, with prior probability P_1, reflecting our degree of confidence in this hypothesis, and hypothesis 2, with prior probability P_2 – our prior odds relating to the two hypotheses work out as P_1/P_2 – say, e.g., one to one. Then, given the observed data, we compute a Bayes factor relating to the two hypotheses that incorporates the information in the data, say, five heads in five tosses. Then we have the general result that the posterior odds relating to the two hypotheses, denoted by K_{12}, is given by $K_{12} = $ Prior Odds × Bayes Factor, where the Bayes factor is given by $\Pr\{r = 5 \mid n = 5, \theta = 1\}/\Pr\{r = 5 \mid n = 5, \theta = \frac{1}{2}\}$. Applying this to the above coin flipping problem or male/female birth problem, we can compute the odds on the hypotheses $H_1: \theta = 1$ versus $H_2: \theta = 1/2$, given the model and data – five heads in five tosses or five male births in five trials. If we begin one to one on the two hypotheses, after processing the data by use of Bayes' theorem we end up with posterior odds of thirty-two to one in favor of $\theta = 1$ versus $\theta = 1/2$. Also, if we compute the odds on $\theta = 1/2$ versus θ uniformly distributed, zero to one, with prior odds one to one, the posterior odds are six to one on $\theta = 1$ versus θ uniformly distributed zero to one. These posterior odds can be employed to choose optimally between or among alternative hypotheses and/or to average estimates and predictions over alternative hypotheses or models – a very important capability in inference, prediction and forecasting, as will be illustrated later.

Or suppose forecasters have made seven incorrect long-run growth forecasts; what is the probability that their next forecast will be incorrect? In connection with this last problem, note that (1) in the 1890s, forecasters were generally very pessimistic about the long-run prospects of the US economy because of the ending of the western frontier expansion; (2) in the Great Depression of the 1930s, many forecasted the end of US capitalism; (3) the forecasts after World War II were generally that the US economy would fall back into the depression of the 1930s; (4) in the 1950s, many forecasted that the Soviet Union, with Sputnik and a growth rate supposedly twice the US rate, would dominate the United States; (5) in the 1960s, many forecasted that the United States would go down in a flaming racial war; (6) in the 1970s, forecasters generally concluded that high energy and resource prices and shortages would prevent continued US economic growth; and (7) growth forecasters pointed to global warming in the 1980s as having a major negative impact on growth. With a record of seven incorrect forecasts in seven trials, what is the probability of an incorrect forecast on the next trial?

1.3   Some canonical problems

Before getting into discussion of additional technical Bayes/non-Bayes issues, I shall consider a few canonical, applied problems that will, I believe, introduce some deep issues quite painlessly, and hopefully provide illumination. First, we have the fundamental problem of golf club selection, which most of us solve heuristically. E.g., in playing a 185-yard hole with a green surrounded by water, do we use a two-iron in an effort to hit the green in one shot, or do we "play it safe" by using a seven-iron to lay up and then chip to the green in an effort to make a reasonable score by lowering the probability of our ball going into the water?[23] To make this decision problem amenable to quantitative analysis, it occurred to me several years ago on a visit to South Africa, where there are many excellent golfers, that it would be helpful to construct table 1.1.

Table 1.1 *Outcomes, probabilities and utilities associated with use of a two- or seven-iron tee shot on a par three hole*

			Outcomes				
Club	1	2	3	4	5	6[a]	Expected scores and utilities
Two-iron							
Probabilities	p_1	p_2	p_3	p_4	p_5	p_6	$ES_2 = \sum_{i=1}^{6} p_i i$
Utilities	$U_2(1)$	$U_2(2)$	$U_2(3)$	$U_2(4)$	$U_2(5)$	$U_2(6)$	$EU_2 = \sum_{i=1}^{6} p_i U_2(i)$
Seven-iron							
Probabilities	q_1	q_2	q_3	q_4	q_5	q_6	$ES_7 = \sum_{i=1}^{6} q_i i$
Utilities	$U_7(1)$	$U_7(2)$	$U_7(3)$	$U_7(4)$	$U_7(5)$	$U_7(6)$	$EU_7 = \sum_{i=1}^{6} q_i U_7(i)$

[a] Any score higher than a triple bogey, i.e. a 6, is recorded as a 6.

In this table, the possible outcomes for each club selection have been indicated and the p's and q's are the probabilities associated with outcomes. For example, if a two-iron is the club selected, the probability of scoring a hole in one – a score of one – is p_1, while, if a seven-iron is used, the probability of scoring a one is q_1. For the average golfer, it is undoubtedly the case that both of these probabilities are very small in value, with the latter being smaller and quite close to zero. Given the assessed or guessed values of the probabilities, it is direct to compute the expected scores associated with the choices of a two-iron and a seven-iron, denoted by $E\,S_2$ and $E\,S_7$ in the table. Further, if the golfer's loss function is monotonically increasing in expected score, he/she will choose the club with the associated lower expected score, e.g. the two-iron if $E\,S_2 < E\,S_7$. For other loss functions, an optimal choice can be made by choosing the club with an associated lower expected loss. Good luck!

While many variants of the above problem can be analyzed, for present purposes it is relevant to say a few words about the p's and the q's, the probabilities in table 1.1. What are they? How are their values determined? And are they useful?

As regards the p's and q's in table 1.1, I consider them to be quantitative measures of degrees of belief in propositions, e.g. the belief that, if I select a two-iron, my score will be three – say, $p_3 = 0.2$. This is a value that reflects my background information regarding past performance, current conditions and other factors, i.e. a "degree of confidence" concept of probability is being employed here, which is used extensively in science. Clearly, it is not a "long-run frequency" probability *à la* Venn and others since, in the present case, and many others, it is difficult to perform an infinite number (or even a very large number) of repetitions of the "experiment" under identical conditions because players age and repetitions are rarely "exactly the same." And the relevance of a "hypothetical" experiment in the present context is questionable. Further, it is difficult to interpret the probabilities in table 1.1 as "axiomatic probabilities." Here there are six possible outcomes associated with each club selection and it is unclear how the axiomatic definition can be employed to produce useful probabilities. On an "equally probable" assumption, all the p's would equal 1/6. Would that the probability of a hole in one were equal to 1/6!

Thus, I and many others find the "degree of confidence" concept of probability useful and operational in the present problem and in the general problems encountered in scientific investigations and decision-making. It should also be noted that information on scores in previous rounds of play can be formally combined with our judgmental information using Bayesian methods. For a very useful and penetrating discussion of alternative definitions of probability, see Jeffreys,[24] and note that most statistics and econometrics textbooks do not treat this definitional problem very well, if at all. Thus, many statisticians and econometricians make probability statements that they find hard to interpret satisfactorily. To illustrate, a graduate student once asked me, "Do I have to imagine that God runs the US economy through a historical period over and over again to make probability statements using time series data, as my undergraduate instructor stated?"

Some other problems that are very important and illustrate well the usefulness of the "degree of confidence" concept of probability are "selection" problems. For example, many years ago I asked a dean how he decided how many offers of admission, N, to make to his school each year. He answered that, if he wanted 200 students in his entering class, he would make 400 offers of admission – a "rule of thumb" that he claimed "worked well."

Note that, for a given N, it is direct to compute the expected number and the expected total outlay. If each probability were equal to 1/2, then the dean's "rule of thumb" would apply – that is, $N^e = (1/2)N$. However, additional information regarding individual candidates is usually available, which can be used to assign "more realistic" values to the probabilities and thus more realistic estimates of the expected number enrolling and the expected outlays on fellowship awards. Also,

Table 1.2 *Candidates for admission, awards, probabilities of acceptance, and expected enrollment and outlays*

Candidate	Fellowship award	Probability of acceptance	Expected outlay
1	A_1	P_1	$P_1 A_1$
2	A_2	P_2	$P_2 A_2$
.	.	.	.
.	.	.	.
.	.	.	.
N	A_N	P_N	$P_N A_N$
Expected values	$N^e = \sum_1^N P_i$	$A^e = \sum_1^N P_i A_i$	

in a paper by Marsh and me,[25] it is explained how to obtain the optimal number of offers to make so as to have the number accepting close to a target number – say, N^* – using symmetric and asymmetric loss functions.[26] Also, past data and statistical models – e.g. logit or probit models – can be employed to obtain more informative probabilities for solving this and other problems. And, most important, actual enrollments can be compared to forecasted enrollments year by year to determine the quality of the procedure and possibly improve it.

The above problem is similar to those involved in planning parties, meetings, seating on airplanes, hotel room reservations, etc. See references in our paper.[27] Here, as in the earlier golf problem, the "degree of confidence" concept of probability is very useful and easy to interpret. As an "exercise," try to interpret the probabilities in table 1.2 in terms of long-run frequencies or axiomatically.

Another important problem that lends itself well to Bayesian solution is the optimal portfolio problem. We have m assets each with their own future return and we wish to form an optimal portfolio. Let y_{if} denote the return on the i'th asset in the future period f and assume that $y_{if} = x_{if}' \beta_i + u_{if}$ is the relation between the return, some input variables, x_{if}, and an error term with β_i a vector of parameters with unknown values. The return on the portfolio in period f is $R_f = w_1 y_{1f} + w_2 y_{2f} + \cdots + w_m y_{mf}$, where w_i is the investment in the i'th asset. Given a utility function for returns, $U(R_f)$, and a predictive density for R_f, it is possible to maximize expected utility $EU(R_f) = \int U(R_f) f(R_f \mid D) \, dR_f$, where D denotes past data and prior information with respect to the values of the w_i's, subject to the condition that they add up to initial wealth, i.e. $W_o = \sum w_i$. The solution to this problem is the optimal portfolio $w^* = (w_1^*, w_2^*, \ldots, w_m^*)$.

Note that the optimal values of the w's above are just functions of the data and past prior information. In early work on the portfolio problem by Markowitz and others,[28] the "optimal" w's were derived using the sampling density of the y's that depends on nuisance parameters, e.g. the regression coefficients, error term variances and covariances, etc. Substituting estimates of the values of these nuisance parameters in the expressions for the "optimal" w's led to poor approximations to the optimizing values, as shown in the work of Brown and others.[29] By integrating out the nuisance parameters to derive the predictive density, denoted by $f(R_f \mid D) = \int h(R_f \mid \theta, D) g(\theta \mid D) \, d\theta$, where h is the sampling density for R_f given the nuisance parameters θ and D, the past data and prior information, and g is the posterior density for θ. Here the ability to integrate out nuisance parameters is not only useful but also profitable. For further material on Bayesian portfolio analysis and applications, including multi-period problems employing models with time-varying parameters and multivariate shrinkage estimation techniques that are employed on Wall Street and elsewhere, see articles by Putnam, Quintana and others in the annual Proceedings Volumes of the Bayesian Statistical Science Section of the American Statistical Association.[30]

There are many other decision and control problems, including those that have been put forward by Tinbergen and many others, concerned with policy issues that have been solved as simply as those above using the Bayesian approach, whereas only approximate non-Bayesian solutions are available.[31] In the simplest versions of these problems, we have a target value of a variable, Y^*, an assumed percent rate of growth of GDP, a policy control variable – say, the rate of growth of money, M – and a relation connecting Y to M, $Y = Mv + u$, where v is a positive parameter and u is an error term. If we use squared error loss, $L = c(Y - Y^*)^2$, where c is a positive constant, we can evaluate expected loss and find the minimizing value of M. That is, $EL = cE(vM + u - Y^*)^2 = c(M^2 Ev^2 - 2MY^* Ev + Y^{*2} + Eu^2)$. On minimizing this last expression with respect to M, the optimal value is $M^* = (Ev/Ev^2)Y^* = (Y^*/Ev)[1/(1 + \text{var } v)/(Ev)^2)]$. It is seen that the optimal setting for M is equal to the target value for Y, Y^*, divided by the mean of v, Y^*/Ev, times a factor $1/[1 + \text{var } v/(Ev)^2]$ that reflects the spread of the posterior distribution of the parameter v. Note that the above solution is usually obtained using a posterior distribution for v based on past data and prior information. If no past data are available, the solution can also be obtained using just a prior density. In contrast, a non-Bayesian, "certainty equivalence" solution to the problem involves minimizing the expectation of the above loss function given the value of the parameter v, to obtain $M^{ce} = Y^*/v$, and then inserting an estimate of v – say, a least squares estimate – to obtain an "operational" solution, $\hat{M}^{ce} = Y^*/\hat{v}$. Note that assuming $v = \hat{v}$ takes no account of the precision with which the parameter has been estimated, the estimation risk, and thus, as shown in the literature, the certainty equivalence solution is sub-optimal relative to the Bayesian solution.[32]

More complicated policy problems have been analyzed in the Bayesian literature. One that is very important, as Tinbergen recognized, is the choice of the social welfare function or social loss function, assumed to be quadratic in the simple example considered in the previous paragraph. Now, it may be asked, "Is the 4 percent target rate of growth an accurate target?" Perhaps it is too high or too low. Similarly, if there are costs associated with changing the money supply variable, they have to be evaluated to formulate the social loss function. As with the target growth rate, such costs of change can be overstated or understated – another example of loss function misspecification. A very important question is, "What are the effects of such possible errors in formulating social loss or welfare functions?" In an article written for a Tinbergen *festschrift* volume, I used Bayesian methods to analyze such problems and found that (1) overstating costs of change and overstating the target growth rate, Y* above, can be exactly off-setting errors, whereas, on the other hand, (2) underestimating the cost of changing M and overstating the target growth rate Y* were found to be reinforcing errors. That is, with an erroneously low cost of changing the policy variable M, it was changed too much in an effort to reach a mistakenly high target value Y*. Whether the errors in (1) or in (2) are made more frequently by politicians on the right or on the left is a key problem deserving more analysis.

1.4   Bayes – non-Bayes issues

Having considered briefly some canonical problems, let us now turn to take up some of the basic issues involved in the Bayes – non-Bayes controversy about how to conduct our primary activities of learning from data and making decisions. This controversy has raged for more than two centuries since the publication of Bayes' paper in 1763 and is currently being resolved in what Kuhn would call a paradigm shift in statistics, econometrics, forecasting and other fields. In table 1.3 is a summary listing of questions relating to a number of central issues and Bayesian and non-Bayesian responses that I consider reasonably accurate and put forward for your consideration.

In what follows, I shall review the questions and answers in table 1.3 with discussions that I hope you will find helpful. To be perfectly frank, I have indicated my personal conclusion at the bottom of the table. Hopefully, these considerations will be helpful in clarifying issues and providing further information. We shall start with issue 1 and proceed one by one to consider others on the list.

Table 1.3 *Bayes – non-Bayes issues*

Issues	Answers	
	Bayes	non-Bayes
1 Uses a formal learning model?	Yes	No
2 Axiomatic support?	Yes	?
3 Probabilities associated with hypotheses	Yes	No
4 Probability defined as a degree of confidence in a proposition?	Yes	No
5 Uses $\Pr\{a < \beta < b \text{ given data}\}$?	Yes	No
6 Uses $\Pr\{c < y_f < d \text{ given data}\}$?	Yes	No
7 Minimization of Bayes risk?	Yes	No
8 Uses prior distributions?	Yes	?
9 Uses subjective prior information?	Yes	Yes
10 Integrates out nuisance parameters?	Yes	No
11 Good asymptotic results?	Yes	Yes
12 Exact, good finite sample results?	Yes	Sometimes
Personal conclusion? It pays to go Bayes!		

Issue 1. Learning model?

In answer to the first question in table 1.3, Bayesians use Bayes' theorem as a formal model in learning from data in a reproducible fashion. Non-Bayesians do not use a formal learning model and thus they learn informally from their data. The Bayesian learning model has been applied in analyses of all kinds of problems in statistics, econometrics and other areas and been shown to produce reliable, useful results. Further, various rationalizations of the Bayesian learning model using probability theory and information theory have appeared in the literature. For example, as noted above, using information theory, I[33] have shown that Bayes' theorem can be derived as the solution to an optimization problem, namely minimization of the difference between measures of the output information and the input information with respect to the form of the output or post data density for the parameters. Also, it is a 100 percent efficient information processing rule. However, this is not to say that the traditional Bayesian learning model cannot be improved and extended. Indeed, various extensions and modifications of Bayes' rule have appeared in work by Dempster, Diaconis, Hill, Just, me and others.[34] One might say that Bayes' rule is the "Model T" learning model that works quite well. However, past and current research is directed at extending and improving it to permit a wider range of learning problems to be solved satisfactorily or optimally, e.g. learning under conditions of ignorance or without a prior density, as R. A. Fisher wished to do in his fiducial approach,[35] and dynamic learning problems involving costs associated with changing beliefs and acquiring new information.

Issue 2. Axiom systems?

As regards issue 2 in table 1.3, there are quite a few axiom systems underlying the Bayesian approach, e.g. those of Jeffreys, Savage, de Finetti and others. While they differ in certain important respects and certainly are not "perfect," they do exist and give evidence of much hard thought regarding fundamental considerations. As regards axiom systems for non-Bayesian approaches, I do not know of any. It appears that non-Bayesians approach inference in an artful way.

Issues 3 and 4. Probabilities associated with hypotheses to express degrees of confidence?

With respect to issues 3 and 4 in table 1.3, Bayesians along with many others associate probabilities with hypotheses or propositions to represent degrees of confidence in such propositions. For example, it is considered useful and meaningful for a forecaster to state that the probability that the economy will turn down in the next quarter is equal to 0.3 – a value that reflects his or her available information. Or a forecaster may state the odds of two to one on the Bank of England's macroeconomic model versus a competing hypothesized model to reflect relative degrees of confidence in the alternative models. Many regard the failure of other definitions of probability to accommodate probabilities associated with hypotheses as a major defect of such definitions, e.g. the long-run frequency, axiomatic, hypothetical infinite population, etc. definitions. In the Bayesian approach, such probabilities and odds are not only used but are formally updated, using Bayes' theorem, as new information becomes available. For example, in forecasting, the probabilities of hypothesized, alternative movements – e.g. downturn or no downturn, in the rate of growth of real GDP for next year – have been utilized to determine optimal turning point forecasts; see, e.g., my paper with C. Min with applications to forecasting turning points in eighteen countries' annual growth rates (a response to Milton Friedman), and references to the earlier literature cited therein.[36] In contrast, the probability concepts employed by non-Bayesians do *not* permit them to associate probabilities with hypotheses, e.g. the probability associated with the hypothesis that economic activity will turn down next quarter, even though they often do so in practice.

Thus, in testing hypotheses, non-Bayesians cannot formally consider or evaluate the probabilities or odds on alternative hypotheses or models – a very severe limitation on the learning process. In this connection, it should be appreciated that "likelihoods" or "likelihood ratios" are not "probabilities" or "ratios of probabilities," as is well known, even though some practitioners confuse these concepts. It is indeed interesting to note that bookmakers and insurance companies have no difficulty in using odds and probabilities. For some pioneering early uses of Bayesian analysis in the insurance industry, see the review paper by R. Miller.[37] And, for an account of the use of Bayesian analysis to understand how Lloyds of London issued a policy to insure the Cutty Sark company for risk associated with its public offer of £1 million for the capture of the Loch Ness monster, see the amusing paper by Karl Borch.[38]

Thus, being able to assign and update probabilities associated with hypotheses and models in the Bayesian approach is very useful not only in learning from data but also in choosing between or among alternative hypotheses and models. Further, these probabilities have been employed to average or combine alternative models and their forecasts. See the article by Min and me[39] for formulation and applications of optimal Bayesian model and forecast combining techniques, which are compared to various non-Bayesian forecast combining techniques due to Bates, Granger and others, where it was found that Bayesian methods performed somewhat better than non-Bayesian methods.[40]

Last, it should be appreciated that Bayesian methods for analyzing and choosing between or among alternative hypotheses when "Knightian uncertainty" or "ignorance" is present have been considered in the literature, and this is, I believe, fertile ground for much additional research. For example, with "ignorant" participants in financial markets, how does their performance compare to markets with "fully informed, rational" participants? Behavioral financial economists and others are asking questions such as these but have not as yet, to my knowledge, produced a reliable model that explains variation in past data, predicts well and is useful in forming portfolios that yield good or average rates of return.

Issue 5. Probability interval for a parameter

Next, we consider item 5 in table 1.3, namely the simple probability statement that the value of a parameter, denoted by θ, lies between two given values, a and b. For example, this might be the probability that the marginal propensity to consume (MPC) lies between 0.60 and 0.80 given our past data and information. Bayesians easily interpret and compute such probabilities. However, non-Bayesians do not or cannot. For example, if 0.60 to 0.80 is a 95 percent non-Bayesian confidence interval for the MPC, it is incorrect to say that the probability is 0.95 that the value of the MPC lies between 0.60 and 0.80. Rather, one should say that 0.60 to 0.80 is the realized value of a random interval that, if computed over and over again, has a probability of 0.95 of covering the true MPC. Also, when it comes to using sample data to estimate population characteristics – e.g. a national unemployment rate, or the percentage of the voting population favoring a particular candidate – many times an estimate (say, 45.2 percent in favor of a particular candidate) is accompanied by a statement such as: "The margin of error is 3.1 percentage points" – a statement and number, 3.1, that many have difficulty understanding. A statement such as: "To the best of our knowledge, the probability is 0.90 that the percentage of the voting population favoring candidate A is between 42 and 48 percent" is a much more informative and easily understood statement.

Thus, there is a fundamental difference in the interpretation of Bayesian and frequentist, non-Bayesian intervals, even when they numerically coincide. In the special cases in which the intervals are numerically the same, then the Bayesian interval often has both a posterior degree of belief interpretation and the non-Bayesian frequentist, say, 95 percent coverage property. The latter is a useful property in appraising "operating characteristics" of a procedure whereas the former is more appropriate for making inferences in a specific situation with given data. Of practical importance too are the many problems – e.g. forecasting time series problems – for which exact, finite sample frequentist intervals are not available and use is made of approximate, large sample approximate intervals, whereas with the Bayesian approach exact finite sample intervals can be and have been computed.

Issue 6. Predictive intervals?

The next item, item 6, in table 1.3 relates to interpretations of Bayesian and non-Bayesian predictive intervals, and involves issues similar to those considered above in connection with alternative confidence intervals. Years ago, I made the statement that very few know how to interpret non-Bayesian prediction intervals. In response to a challenge to my statement, I asked a number of colleagues and graduate students to interpret the following statement: "A 95 percent non-Bayesian prediction interval for next year's rate of growth of real GDP for the US economy is, numerically, 1.0 percent to 3.0 percent." About 70 percent of the respondents could not satisfactorily interpret this prediction interval. One respondent told me that it means that the probability is 0.95 that next year's rate of growth will be between 1.0 percent and 3.0 percent. He did not realize that he had given me the standard Bayesian interpretation of the interval, not the non-Bayesian interpretation, which is as follows. The interval 1.0 percent to 3.0 percent is the realized value of a random interval that has probability 0.95 of covering or including next year's as yet unobserved random growth rate. Imagine how the President of the United States or the Prime Minister of the United Kingdom would respond to such a "clarifying" statement, which is more a property of a procedure than a direct measure of the uncertainty involved in prediction or forecasting.

Predictive densities for one or more future observations are easily derived in the Bayesian approach and are used to compute predictive intervals as well as optimal point predictions. That is, given a predictive loss function, it is direct to derive the optimal forecast that minimizes expected loss. For example, with a quadratic loss function the predictive mean is an optimal point prediction, while for an absolute error loss function the median of the predictive density is an optimal point prediction. For useful asymmetric loss functions, optimal point predictions that differ considerably from those that are optimal relative to symmetric loss functions have been derived and are easily computed in applications; see, e.g., the pioneering work by Varian and later papers extending his work.[41]

Further, the predictive density is very important in solving various control and decision problems, including economic policy-making problems, portfolio problems, etc., as noted above. Also, as mentioned earlier, the Bayesian approach has been useful in studying how errors in formulating social welfare or loss functions affect solutions to public policy and other problems. That many business, medical, engineering, economic policy and other problems can be readily solved using Bayesian methods is indeed fortunate and important.

Last, predictive densities are very useful in connection with forming optimal portfolios and managing risk in the financial world.[42] Given that the return on a portfolio is a linear combination of individual asset returns, the predictive density of the portfolio return has been derived and used to determine optimal portfolio weights, summing to initial wealth, that maximize the expected utility of the portfolio return, as mentioned above. In work by Brown, non-normal return distributions were employed in solving for optimal Bayesian portfolios.[43] Jorion employed Stein shrinkage techniques in his predictive analyses and derivation of optimal portfolios while Quintana et al. employed Bayesian state space, time-varying parameter (TVP) models, "seemingly unrelated regression" (SUR) and "shrinkage" estimation and prediction techniques in solving for optimal portfolios month by month in a sequential, optimal fashion.[44] In experimental calculations, their procedures produced cumulative returns that compared very favorably with those associated with the Standard & Poor's 500 portfolio. A growing number of financial firms on Wall Street and elsewhere have been using Bayesian predictive densities and methods for a number of years. Also, various uses of Bayesian predictive densities and methods at Microsoft have been described by Heckerman.[45]

Issue 7. Minimization of Bayes risk?

In item 7 in table 1.3 it is indicated that Bayesians minimize Bayes risk, when it exists and is finite, in choosing estimators while non-Bayesians do not. The difference arises because non-Bayesians do not employ prior densities for parameters that are required to define Bayes risk. That is, given a convex loss function, $L(\theta, \hat{\theta})$, where θ is a parameter to be estimated and $\hat{\theta}$ is some estimator, the usual risk function is $r(\theta) = \int L(\theta, \hat{\theta}) f(y \mid \theta) d\theta$, where $f(y \mid \theta)$ is the data density. Since different estimators have different risk functions that often cross, one cannot use their associated risks functions to choose among them. Average risk (AR) or Bayes' risk (BR) is defined to be $BR = \int \pi(\theta) r(\theta) d\theta$, where $\pi(\theta)$ is a prior density and the integral is assumed to converge. As shown in Bayesian statistics and econometrics texts, when the integral defining AR converges to a finite value the optimal Bayesian estimate (obtained by minimizing posterior expected loss), viewed as an estimator, minimizes AR and thus is admissible. That is, given that the Bayesian estimator minimizes AR, there cannot be another that has uniformly lower risk, $r(\theta)$, over the entire parameter space since it would have lower BR than the estimator, which minimizes average risk – a contradiction. Thus Bayesians can obtain optimal estimators that minimize Bayes' risk in this way, whereas non-Bayesians cannot since they do not use prior distributions that are needed to define average or Bayes' risk.[46]

Issues 8 and 9. Prior distributions and subjective prior information?

On the use of prior distributions, issue 8 in table 1.3, it is the case that Bayesians use prior densities, both "non-informative" and "informative," whereas non-Bayesians state that they do not, and this has been a bone of contention for many years. In recent years, since the introduction of the Bayesian method of moments (BMOM) in the early 1990s, it has become possible to perform inverse inference without introducing a prior density or a likelihood function in many different, commonly encountered problems, e.g. location, regression, multivariate regression, time series, dichotomous random variable and other models.[47]

As an example of the BMOM, assume that we have observed times to failure in n cases and that the observed times satisfy the relation $y_i = \theta + u_i$, $i = 1, 2, \ldots$, n, where the y_i's are given observations, θ is a non-negative parameter with an unknown value and the u_i's are realized, unobserved error terms. If we sum both sides and divide by n, we have, for the mean of y, $\overline{y} = \theta + \overline{u}$, where $\overline{u} = \Sigma u_i / n$, the mean of the realized error terms. On taking the subjective expectation of both sides of this last equation with $\overline{y}$ having a given known value, $\overline{y} = E\theta + E\overline{u}$. Now, if we assume that there are no outliers, no left-out variables and that the relation is appropriately formulated, we can assume that the post data expectation $E\overline{u} = 0$ that implies from the relation above that $E\theta = \overline{y}$. Thus, we have the value of a post data mean of the parameter θ obtained without a prior density, likelihood function or Bayes' theorem. Note that the above assumption regarding the mean of the realized error terms appears much weaker than iid, normal, zero mean, common variance sampling assumptions about error terms that are usually made to obtain normal likelihood functions. We can also solve for the most spread out, or least informative, proper density for θ – say, $g(\theta \mid y)$ – with the above given mean $\overline{y}$ by choosing it to minimize $\int g(\theta \mid y) \log g(\theta \mid y) \, d\theta$; that is, minimize the average log height or negative entropy relative to uniform measure. The solution is the exponential density for θ given the data y; that is, $g^*(\theta \mid y) = (1/\overline{y}) \exp(-\theta/\overline{y})$. Since this density can be employed to compute $\Pr\{a < \theta < b \mid y\}$, the famous inverse problem of Bayes, the procedure to obtain it is called the Bayesian method of moments. In papers in the literature, the BMOM approach, utilizing the above and other assumptions regarding properties of the realized and future, as yet unrealized error terms, has been used to make inverse and predictive inferences in connection with regression, time series and many other models.[48] See also the work of Golan, Judge and Miller, and of Mittelhammer, Judge and Miller, for a somewhat different "generalized maximum entropy" approach for performing inverse inference without sampling assumptions and Bayes' theorem.[49] In recent work, BMOM and traditional Bayesian regression models have been compared using posterior odds and other model comparison techniques.[50]

Note also that non-Bayesians using random effects models and stochastic volatility models assume that parameters are random and introduce densities, e.g. normal densities, for random effects and stochastic processes for volatility parameters. Also, in random parameter regression and time series state space models, parameters are considered to be random and forms for their densities are assumed. These assumed densities for parameters are much like prior densities in traditional Bayesian analyses and are well known to incorporate additional, non-sample information in analyses. Good has noted that this may be a basis for a Bayes / non-Bayes compromise.[51] However, non-Bayesians often remark that their parameter densities are "part of the model," not prior densities. While this is a thin distinction, there can be no doubt but that non-Bayesians are adding prior information by introducing probability density functions for parameters. Whether the added information in prior densities is justified or not cannot be settled deductively but must be settled empirically in terms of model comparison techniques and predictive performance.

With respect to the aforementioned capability of comparing BMOM and traditional Bayesian models, the eminent British statistician George A. Barnard wrote in a private communication in 1997:

> And above all any method is welcome which, unlike nonparametrics, remains fully quantifiable without paying obeisance to a model which one knows is false. And your proposal to compare BMOM results with a model-based one should achieve the best of both worlds.

> The general point seems to me to be that we should express prior knowledge, as far as we can, in a prior. Then our model – likelihood-producing or moment-producing, or whatever – should help us

process the observed data. Then we should go back to compare what we thought we knew before with the result of our data processing. In arriving at our (for the time being) conclusion the weight that we attach to the three components of our inference will vary from case to case. BMOM will be specially useful when the latter two stages of the three should predominate.

It should also be recognized that choice of a functional form for a relation usually involves a lot of prior information, as many have recognized. For example, if we choose to employ a Cobb-Douglas production function, we should realize that it implies a non-U-shaped long-run average cost function unless a fixed cost of entry is added to other costs. Or, if we choose to formulate the demand function for real money, M, as $\log M = a - br + \ldots$, where b is a positive parameter and r is an interest rate, this relation implies that money demand will be more elastic at high than at low levels of r, contrary to what Keynesians believe. Perhaps use of $1/r$ rather than r would satisfy Keynesians. Also, some have used a log-log relation for the murder rate, m and the execution rate, x (that is, $\log m = a - b \log x + \cdots$) without noting that with $b > 0$ such a relation predicts that, as the execution rate, x, approaches zero, *ceteris paribus*, the murder rate, m, shoots off to infinity! Perhaps a semi-logarithmic relation would be more sensible given that in some states of the United States $x = 0$. Thus, in these cases and many more that could be cited, choice of a functional form for a relation or a density function for error terms involves a good deal of prior information with respect to what is "reasonable" and what is not. Note that normal error term densities have very thin tails and constant variances and thus are, as is well known, inappropriate for stock return data and are often replaced by Student-t or other densities that can have heavy tails, along with processes for error term variances – for example ARCH, GARCH and stochastic volatility models of various kinds.[52] Further, sometimes we know, as in the case of intra-day stock price changes, that distributions can be skewed and sometimes bimodal; for such situations, unimodal, symmetric densities are not appropriate, and some have employed exponential quartic densities that can be skewed and/or bimodal. Obviously, such prior information about distributions underlying likelihood functions is very important, and failing to take good account of it can obviously lead to serious inference errors, poorly fitting relations, bad forecasts and poor portfolios.

Thus, in summary, non-Bayesians as well as Bayesians use and misuse prior information and require use of good model comparison and predictive checks to determine what prior information and models to use in practice.

Issue 10. Integrating out nuisance parameters?

On the issue of integrating out nuisance parameters, number 10 in table 1.3, Bayesians have utilized this option extensively whereas non-Bayesians have not. As shown above, it is direct for Bayesians to integrate out nuisance parameters to obtain the marginal densities of parameters of interest and also to use conditional posterior densities to explore the sensitivity of inferences about parameters of interest to what is assumed about the nuisance parameters' values. In contrast, in non-Bayesian approaches, this capability of integrating out nuisance parameters is not available and often nuisance parameters are replaced by estimates in expressions for optimal estimators, e.g. generalized least squares (GLS) estimators, which often depend on parameters of covariance matrices. The resulting, so-called "feasible" GLS estimators are justified asymptotically in terms of consistency and asymptotic normality and efficiency. However, the small sample properties of such "feasible" or "operational" approximately optimal estimators constitute a key issue. In some cases, as is well known, asymptotically optimal estimators have rather poor small sample properties. On the contrary, Bayesian estimates have finite sample and large sample optimal properties in terms of minimizing expected loss. As regards Bayesian estimators, as pointed out above, in many cases they are the estimators that minimize Bayes' risk and are admissible when Bayes' risk is finite. In some cases, particularly when diffuse, improper priors are employed, there is no assurance that Bayesian estimates that minimize expected loss are admissible. However, given the minimal prior information employed, it is doubtful that other estimators, based on just the minimal information employed, are uniformly better. In the classic Stein inadmissibility results, it should be appreciated that he employed an informative prior density for his means in his Bayesian derivation of his famous shrinkage estimates.[53]

Issues 11 and 12. Asymptotic and finite sample properties?

With respect to item 11 in table 1.3, generally Bayesian and non-Bayesian methods have good asymptotic properties with respect to models with a fixed number of parameters. Years ago, Jeffreys showed under rather general conditions that, in large samples, posterior densities assume a normal shape centered at the maximum likelihood estimate, with a covariance matrix given by the inverse of the estimated Fisher information matrix, and interpreted this result as a justification for the method of maximum likelihood. Later, Heyde and Johnstone, and Chen, showed that the conditions needed for the asymptotic normality of maximum likelihood estimators and of Bayesian posterior densities are identical when observations are stochastically independent. However, in the case of stochastically dependent observations, the conditions required for the asymptotic normality of posterior densities are simpler than those required for the asymptotic normality of maximum likelihood estimators.[54]

As regards finite sample situations, non-Bayesian procedures many times do not have good finite sample properties. This is particularly true for testing, estimation and prediction procedures for simultaneous equations, non-linear, time series, discrete random variable and many other commonly encountered models. For example, in terms of the widely employed simultaneous equations model with normal error terms, which can be viewed as a linear multivariate regression model subject to non-linear restrictions (as in the pioneering work of Anderson and Rubin[55]), the maximum likelihood estimators put forward by them have been shown not to possess finite moments in general and have heavy-tailed densities. As pointed out in later work, in the canonical form of the model the estimation problem is one of estimating a ratio of parameters.[56] A similar ratio estimation problem is encountered in the widely used Nerlove agricultural supply model, where a key parameter, the coefficient of anticipated price, in the supply function is algebraically linked to the reduced form regression parameters as follows: $\alpha = b_1/(1 - b_2 - b_3)$, where the b's are reduced form coefficients. As mentioned in Diebold and Lamb, when least squares estimators are substituted for the b's, the resulting estimator for α has a rather heavy-tailed density, without finite moments that can be bimodal.[57] For other such examples involving failure of moments to exist and bimodal densities for estimators, see papers by Nelson and Startz, me, and others.[58]

In Monte Carlo experiments conducted by Diebold and Lamb and Shen and Perloff, it is shown that Bayesian and certain BMOM and generalized maximum entropy (GME) estimators have much better small sample properties than the widely used "plug-in" estimator for α described above. Also, see papers by Tsurumi, Park, Gao and Lahiri, Shen and Perloff, and Zellner for additional Monte Carlo evidence showing that Bayesian estimators for parameters of simultaneous equations models perform better than maximum likelihood, modified maximum likelihood, two-stage least squares, ordinary least squares and other estimators. In particular, traditional Bayesian and BMOM estimates, which are optimal relative to an extended, two-part, balanced loss function, with one term reflecting goodness of fit and the second precision of estimation, performed exceptionally well in the Monte Carlo experiments of Tsurumi, and Gao and Lahiri.[59] In addition to providing good point estimates, as mentioned above in the Bayesian, BMOM or GME approaches, the complete exact finite sample post data densities for parameters and predictive densities for future observations are available, some obtained by employing "direct" Monte Carlo techniques and others by use of Markov Chain Monte Carlo (MCMC) techniques. For more on the powerful impact MCMC and related numerical techniques are having on Bayesian analysis, see review articles and references in the December 2000 issue of the *Journal of the American Statistical Association* (JASA) and the 1996 article by Chib and Greenberg. Also, it should be recognized that, in recent work, Dufour and Khalaf have used related numerical integration procedures in an effort to improve non-Bayesian, sampling theory approaches to estimation, prediction and other inference techniques.[60]

Personal conclusion?

From the above summary overview, and from the many impressive Bayesian applied analyses that have been performed over the years in many different fields, I have personally concluded that "It pays to go Bayes!" This should not be interpreted to mean that no further progress is possible or needed. Indeed, as reported in Soofi's JASA review article,[61] there are new developments in information theory that are very relevant for work in statistics, econometrics and forecasting. For example, as mentioned earlier, a new procedure for producing optimal information processing rules, including Bayes' theorem and variants of it, is available. Briefly, the procedure involves consideration of input and output information. The problem to be solved is how to choose an output density for the parameters so as to have the output information as close as possible to the input information. We want the output information to be as close as possible to the input information to avoid losing information. On minimizing an information function $\Delta(g)$, with respect to the choice of the form of the output or post data density for the parameters, denoted by g, the optimal choice of g is given by $g^* = \pi l / h$ – that is, the solution is in the form of

Bayes' theorem. Having a new derivation of the traditional Bayesian learning model, namely Bayes' theorem, is important since, as mentioned above, earlier derivations of Bayes' theorem involve certain assumptions that may not be fulfilled in all circumstances, as Jeffreys pointed out many years ago. Further, the new informational approach for generating optimal information processing rules lends itself easily to produce new learning models and generalizations of the traditional Bayesian learning model. For example, as I have shown recently, it is possible to weight the information in the prior density differently from that in the likelihood function and, when this is done, the optimal solution, denoted by g^{**}, is given by $g^{**} = c\pi^{w_1}l^{w_2}$, where w_1 and w_2 are the weights associated with the inputs and c is a normalizing constant. Further, it is possible to input just a likelihood function and *no* prior, as R. A. Fisher wished to do in his fiducial inference approach. When this is done, the optimal information processing rule is to take the output density g proportional to the likelihood function. Further, dynamic versions of the information processing problem have been formulated in which information output of one period and new data are inputs to the following period and the dynamic information processing problem is in the form of a dynamic programming problem. On minimizing the criterion functional *à la* Bellman, the optimal sequential solution was found to be to update period by period by use of the traditional Bayes' rule, and, when this is done, output information = input information – that is, the process is 100 percent efficient. However, when costs of changing beliefs are introduced, the solution is not in the form of Bayes' theorem but close to the form of empirical learning models derived in the psychological literature from experimental learning experiments, e.g. the Hogarth and Einhorn belief adjustment model.[62] Thus, optimal information processing rules, including Bayes' theorem as a special case, are available for general use in scientific induction to help scientists to learn more effectively from their data.

With these remarks made about methods, I now turn to discuss some specific aspects of forecasting and its role in econometrics and statistics.

1.5   The role of forecasting in econometrics and statistics

It is a fact that not many econometrics textbooks discuss forecasting and indeed many economists seem to show a strong aversion to the topic, perhaps because it is "a-theoretical," "too empirical," and/or "too dangerous." That is, many economists and econometricians concentrate their attention on creating causal models that "explain" and "predict." For example, using the laws of demand and supply, one can predict the probable effects of the imposition of a tax on the price of a product with an associated causal explanation that is rather dependable. However, in other areas where no dependable causal laws are available, many use empirical relations, sometimes time series models, that have little economic or other subject matter justification to "forecast" future outcomes, e.g. next year's rate of growth of real GDP or a downturn in the economy. Thus, forecasting models, without subject matter theoretical support from, e.g., the dependable laws of demand and supply (whether in economics, meteorology, geology or other areas), are distinguished from what econometricians, statisticians and others call "structural" or "causal" models. Ideally, we would like to have structural or causal models that explain and predict outcomes very well. However, particularly in the macroeconomics area, unfortunately, it has been difficult to formulate such dependable models; for more discussion of this range of issues, see the thoughtful article by Ray Fair in a conference volume on alternative macroeconomic theories and the evidence supporting them.[63] He concluded that much more testing of alternative theories is needed.

I believe that not many texts emphasize the important role of forecasting and forecasting models in efforts to build "structural" or "causal" econometric models that work well in prediction and explanation. That is, instead of always going from economic theory and tentative structural models to the data, it is often valuable to go from the data and simple empirical forecasting models that work well in practice to efforts to explain theoretically why these empirical, forecasting models are successful. In the structural econometric modeling, time series analysis approach, which first appeared in the literature in the early 1970s, this two-way interaction between economic theory and the data is emphasized.[64] It was recognized that we might have a tentatively formulated structural econometric model. Given the equations of the model – say, a model of an economy – we solve algebraically for the equations explaining the variation of individual variables; so-called "final equations," or "transfer equations." Then we check the forms of these equations against those determined empirically from the data – that is, forecasting models – and also compare the forecasting performance of these tentative SEMs against that of empirical benchmark models – say, simple random walk models or univariate statistical time series models. In many past studies, it has been found that the forecasts of simple univariate time series benchmark models are better than those of complicated SEMs. When such is the case, it is necessary to reformulate a SEM in an effort to get models that perform adequately in forecasting or to build simpler new SEMs. Last, it should not be overlooked that many operating SEMS, as well as empirical time series models, including VARs, are not very good in forecasting turning points in economic activity, as many have recognized from painful past experience in connection with incorrect turning point forecasts. For example, a few years ago, when Ray Fair spoke at the University of Chicago on his very impressive macroeconometric model of the US economy, I asked him whether his model had forecasted the 1990–91 downturn correctly. He replied, "Damn it, Arnold, you had to ask that question. I missed the '90–91 downturn along with everyone else." Indeed, the same, general poor turning point forecasting performance was encountered by others in connection with the 1981–82 downturn and in many other turning point episodes.

   In view of difficulties in obtaining good structural models, many have turned to use empirical, statistical models, e.g. vector autoregressions (or, as I refer to them, "very awful regressions"). Years ago, Litterman demonstrated that an unrestricted VAR for the US economy did not work very well in forecasting. He used seven quarterly macroeconomic variables with six lags on each, e.g. real GDP, unemployment rate, an interest rate, a price index, etc. Note, as I have pointed out many times over the years, each equation of his VAR contains a dependent variable, and $7 \times 6 = 42$ lagged explanatory variables and an intercept. This is like using a regression with forty-two highly correlated independent variables; a severe case of multicollinearity. Also, with just a few years of quarterly data available, the ratio of the number of observations to the number of parameters is rather low. Thus, in forecasting, it is the case that the many imprecisely estimated parameters employed contribute to blowing up the mean squared error of forecast and other measures of forecast error, theoretically and practically. In an effort to deal with this problem, Litterman very ingeniously devised informative prior distributions for the many parameters of his VAR and created what is known as a Bayesian VAR, or BVAR, which performed better in forecasting than the unrestricted VAR. The extra prior information in his prior density served to augment the information in his data to produce improved forecasting results. A version of Litterman's BVAR was used by Sims at the Federal Reserve Bank of Minneapolis until it missed the 1990–91 downturn in the US economy. See the discussion of VARs and BVARs in the *Journal of Business and Economic Statistics* by Steven McNees of the Federal Reserve Bank of Boston and Robert Litterman, who concluded that SEMs, VARs and BVARs do not perform adequately in forecasting.[65] They did not consider turning point forecasting performance of current structural and VAR models that is generally recognized to be very poor.

In view of the generally poor forecasting performance of large-scale structural econometric models since the 1970s, many such models have been abandoned. Recently, Fisher and Whitley, in their article "Macroeconomic models at the Bank of England," wrote:

> The role of macroeconomic models is to encapsulate in quantitative form a description of the economy that can be used as a basis for discussion and analysis of policy issues. Macroeconomic models are

> inevitably approximations. For one thing, there are serious difficulties in measuring economic variables . . . More fundamentally, it is simply not possible to capture more than a few of the myriad aspects of economic behaviour in a single model.[66]

This point of view contrasts markedly with the views of many who, before and after World War II, attempted to build large-scale SEMs of economies for explanation, prediction and policy-making purposes. Most of these large-scale models are no longer in operation because of poor performance, and now many economists and others are seeking new, simpler models that explain and predict well and are useful in policy-making. As mentioned earlier, many favor "sophisticated simplicity" in modeling, in accord with the Jeffreys-Wrinch "simplicity postulate" – namely that simpler models are more likely to provide better predictions and understandable explanations.

As an example of a large-scale, quarterly macroeconometric model of the US economy, consider the Federal Reserve-MIT-PENN model with about 170 equations, many of them non-linear stochastic difference equations. It is difficult to prove that this model has a unique solution. In practical use, solutions are obtained for linearized versions of the model, and it is well known that such linearized solutions may not be good solutions to general non-linear systems. As a simple example, consider a linear labor demand equation and a backward-bending labor supply equation. Generally there are two equilibrium solutions. However, with a local linearization of the system there is just one equilibrium solution. Further, when simulation experiments were done with this model, it was discovered that it had very unusual features.[67] For example, when the model was shocked with large changes in its money variable – unborrowed reserves plus currency – a nominal interest rate assumed negative values and the computer program stopped because it was not possible to compute the logarithm of a negative variable. Also, when the model was put through a great depression – such as that of the 1930s – in simulation experiments, its output variable went down, unemployment went up but short- and long-term interest rates went to about 18 percent and stayed there. Further, wages and prices leveled off and never came down. As regards "on-line performance," I learned that there were great difficulties in explaining the output of the model to policy-makers and that it did not work very well in forecasting. After many years of operating the model, the Federal Reserve authorities decided to discontinue using it some years ago and are still searching for a good model.

1.6 The structural econometric modeling, time series analysis (SEMTSA) approach

To satisfy this need for models that work well, it was suggested in the SEMTSA approach that simple forecasting equations for individual variables, perhaps derived algebraically from tentatively formulated dynamic structural models, be considered and evaluated in terms of fit to past data and in forecasting. Then, economic theory can be employed to explain why the equations perform well and to suggest improvements. That is, having a set of tested components, namely forecasting equations for important variables, the problem is how to combine them to produce a structural, causal model. To begin this line of research in the 1980s, my colleagues and I considered modeling and forecasting rates of growth of real GDP for a sample of nine indus-trialized countries: seven European countries, Canada and the United States.[68] Using annual data, our initial model was an autoregression of order three – AR(3) – for each country: that is, for the i'th coun-try in the t'th year, $y_{it} = \beta_{oi} + \beta_{1i} y_{it-1} + \beta_{2i} y_{it-2} + \beta_{3i} y_{it-3} + \varepsilon_{it}$, $i = 1, 2, \ldots, m, t = 1, 2, \ldots, T$, where the β's are parameters and ε_{it} is an error term. A third-order autoregression was chosen to allow for the possibility of having two imaginary roots of the process associated with an oscillatory component and one real root associated with a local trend. While all this theory was fine, it did not take too long to determine that this AR(3) model did not perform well in one-year-ahead forecasting because it was missing cyclical downturns and upturns in the real GDP growth rates. At the top of the cycle, the AR(3) model generally forecasted continued growth when the economy turned down, and, at the bottom of the cycle, it predicted continued contraction when the economy turned up. The same unsatisfactory performance occurred with benchmark random walk and other benchmark time series models, including Box-Jenkins' ARIMA models.

Given the very obvious problem, it did not take long to remember the famous research of Burns and Mitchell on the properties of business cycles in the United Kingdom, France, Germany and the United States using data going back to the nineteenth century.[69] In this research, they found that two variables tended to lead in the business cycle, namely money and stock prices. As regards explanations for these findings, it occurred to me that a traditional monetarist point of view, emphasizing real balance or Pigou effects, which I had estimated in my published thesis research using quarterly data for the United States and which was later confirmed using British data, probably accounted for the leading role of the money variable. That is, changes in real money affect demand, particularly the demand for durables and services on the part of consumers and producers, which results in increased expenditures with a lag. Similarly, in thinking about information flows and the stock market, it is probably the case that those in the market react to news events – say, war news, or news of an increase in oil prices – much more quickly than those making investment and other decisions in industry and government. With these considerations in mind, the above AR(3) model was reformulated to include the lagged rates of growth of real money, GM, and of real stock prices, SR. In addition, a world stock return variable was introduced to reflect world news events, namely WR, the median of the individual countries' real stock price growth rates, to yield the first variant of our "autoregressive, leading indicator" (ARLI) model:

$$y_{it} = \beta_{oi} + \beta_{1i} y_{it-1} + \beta_{2i} y_{it-2} + \beta_{3i} y_{it-3} + \beta_{4i} G M_{t-1}$$
$$+ \beta_{5i} S R_{it-1} + \beta_{6i} S R_{it-2} + \beta_{7i} W R_{t-1} + u_{it} \qquad (1.4)$$

where $i = 1, 2, \ldots, m, t = 1, 2, \ldots, T$, the β's are parameters and u_{it} is an error term for the i'th country in the t'th year.

The model in equation (1.4) was implemented using annual data for seven European countries, Canada and the United States from the IMF's *International Financial Statistics* database, 1954–73 for fitting and 1974–81 for one-year-ahead forecasts, with estimates updated year by year. Initially, when simple least squares estimates and one-year-ahead least square forecasts (which are also "diffuse prior" Bayesian forecasts) were employed, it was found that there was a considerable improvement in forecasting performance, particularly in the vicinity of turning points in the rates of growth of total real output relative to the benchmark models.

In later work the number of countries involved in the analysis was increased to eighteen and the period of forecast extended. See figure 1.1 for box plots of the data. It is seen that the median growth rates of real GDP, real stock prices and real money exhibit cyclical behavior, with the latter two variables showing a tendency to lead. For example, in the 1973–74 oil crisis period, the median growth rates of real stock prices and of real money turned down in 1973, while that of real GDP turned down in 1974.

The fits of the equation (1.4) to the individual countries' data were good but not "too good," with R^2's ranging from 0.26 to 0.76 for the eighteen countries and a median of 0.56.[70] It should be appreciated that the historical period covered by our data, from the early 1950s to the late 1980s, included several wars, oil crises, the imposition of wage and price controls, changes in world trade policies, etc. No dummy variables or intervention procedures were utilized. It appears that our leading indicator money and stock return variables captured

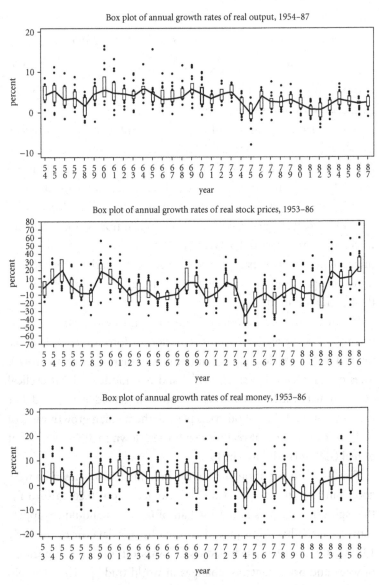

Figure 1.1 Box plot of annual growth rates of real output, real stock prices and real money for eighteen industrialized countries

the effects of many of these major events, although there are some out-
lying points, as shown in figure 1.1. Also, a former student, Chansik
Hong, in his doctoral dissertation studied, among other things, the
dynamic properties of the ARLI model, shown in equation (1.4) for
each of the eighteen countries in our sample.[71] In particular, using
Bayesian methods – namely a normal likelihood function, a diffuse
prior density for the parameters and Bayes' theorem – he computed
the probability that a country's equation has two imaginary roots and
one real root by making draws from the marginal trivariate Student-t
posterior density of the parameters β_{1i}, β_{2i}, and β_{3i} of equation (1.4).
For each draw he computed the roots of the characteristic equation
and found that, in about 85 percent of the draws, he obtained two
complex roots and one real root. Thus, the probability that the process contains an oscillatory component is estimated to be about 0.85.
Further, for those draws leading to imaginary roots, he computed the
period and amplitude of the associated oscillatory component. The
periods so calculated tended to be in the four- to six-year range, and
the amplitudes below one, for each of the eighteen countries. Also, the
real roots of the processes tended to the below one in value. Thus there
appears to be evidence of a damped, oscillatory component and a local,
non-explosive trend in the equations for the eighteen countries.

1.7   Elaborations of the ARLI model

With the simple ARLI model in equation (1.4) formulated for each
country's output growth rate, it was not hard to think about possible modifications that might produce improved performance, just as
Henry Ford did in going from the Model T to the Model A and on
to other models quite successfully. Starting simply and complicating
if necessary seems to be a generally accepted procedure that produces
good results in many areas.

Specifically, with respect to the equation in (1.4), the following
changes were implemented and evaluated in forecasting experiments,

first using data for nine industrialized countries and then eighteen industrialized countries: many European countries, the United States, Canada, Japan and Australia. First, it may be that the coefficients in equation (1.4) are not fixed in value but may vary for a variety of reasons, e.g. aggregation effects, changes in tastes and/or technology, changes in governmental policies, etc. See, e.g., Wolff for evidence that making parameters time-varying in structural exchange rate models led to improved forecasting performance.[72] Thus we allowed the parameters to vary in a variety of ways, using what are called modern Bayesian state space and shrinkage techniques. One simple, state space model allowed the parameter vector in (1.4) to vary through time following a vector random walk. That is, if we write the fixed parameter (FP) version of (1.4) in vector and matrix form as:

$$y_i = X_i \beta_i + u_i, \, i = 1, 2, \ldots, m \qquad (1.5)$$

we assume that the coefficient vector β_i varies through time and follows the following vector random walk process: $\beta_{it} = \beta_{it-1} + e_{it}$, where e_{it} is a white noise error vector. This permits coefficients flexibility to vary in value over different periods and thus to accommodate parameter changes produced by changes in technology or tastes, Lucas effects and other factors producing structural shifts in parameters. Bayesian posterior odds were calculated for fixed versus time-varying parameter models and the results tended to favor time-varying parameters for many countries.[73]

A broader assumption regarding temporal variation in parameters of (1.5) that allows for a Stein shrinkage effect involves assuming $\beta_{it} = \theta_t + v_{it}$ and $\theta_t = \theta_{t-1} + w_t$, with v_{it} and w_t independent white noise error term vectors. Here, in a particular year, the vector β_{it}'s are distributed around a mean vector θ_t, which follows a vector random walk. The Bayesian recursive estimation of these models, which incorporate both shrinkage and time-varying parameter features, was done, and such models were used for forecasting one year ahead, with results that are shown below. As can be seen, it was found that Stein shrinkage was quite important in improving forecast accuracy.

Similar procedures were employed with a slightly elaborated version of our ARLI model in (1.4) to include a world income (WI) variable, $w' = (w_1, w_2, \ldots, w_T)$, the median of the eighteen countries' growth rates, shown in the plots in figure 1. That is, equation (1.4) was elaborated as follows:

$$y_i = X_i \beta_i + w \alpha_i + u_i \qquad (1.6)$$

where $w' = (w_1, w_2, \ldots, w_1, \ldots, w_T)$.

As regards w_t, it was assumed to be generated by the following ARLI equation:

$$w_t = \pi_o + \pi_1 w_{t-1} + \pi_2 w_{t-2} + \pi_3 w_{t-3} + \pi_4 MSR_{t-1}$$
$$+ \pi_5 MGM_{t-1} + \varepsilon_t \qquad (1.7)$$

where MSR_{t-1} = median of the t−1'th year's countries' SRs, and MGM_{t-1} = median of the t−1'th year's real money growth rates and ε_t is an error term. Various versions of the ARLI/WI model in (1.6) and (1.7) were fitted and evaluated in forecasting experiments, including time-varying parameter variants, denoted by TVP/ARLI/WI, with and without shrinkage or pooling.

1.8 Point forecasting results

In table 1.11 are shown the forecasted root mean squared errors (RMSEs) for the eighteen countries, employing fixed and time-varying parameters and with and without pooling or shrinkage. The effects of pooling or shrinkage are striking. In the TVP case, with pooling, the median RMSE = 1.74 percentage points with a minimum RMSE = 1.17 percentage points and a maximum RMSE = 2.53 percentage points, while, without pooling, the median RMSE = 2.37 percentage points with a minimum = 1.39 percentage points and a maximum = 3.32 percentage points. Similarly striking results are encountered in the FP case. Thus the results in table 1.11 show clearly the improvements in forecasting performance produced by use of Bayesian pooling or shrinkage techniques, with results for the time-varying parameter model slightly better than those for the fixed parameter model. Also, it should be appreciated that these models performed much better than various benchmark models, e.g. random walk, AR(3), ARIMA and several other models, in forecasting annual growth rates.

In further efforts to improve performance, in analogy to "continuing product improvement" efforts in industry, we considered procedures for combining or averaging the forecasts of various models. In the extensive literature on combining forecasts, starting with the pioneering Bates-Granger paper in 1969, there has been a belief that combined or averaged forecasts will work better than individual forecasts. Indeed, in some cleverly constructed examples involving consideration of forecasts that are unbiased, it can be shown that combining always pays in terms of increased precision as measured by mean squared error. However, I realized that "always" is a very strong property and that, in life, not all forecasts are unbiased. Indeed, given the poor models used to produce forecasts, it is to be expected that many forecasts will be biased. Further, even with a perfect model, if one uses an asymmetric loss function, it has been shown in the literature that the optimal forecast that minimizes expected loss is biased. For example, if over-forecasting by a given amount is a much more serious error than under-forecasting by the same amount, then a forecast that is biased downward will be optimal. Thus, biased forecasts can be optimal and proofs of the virtues of combining forecasts that are based on the assumption that all forecasts are unbiased are quite limited in their applicability. Another point is that usually these proofs of the optimality of combining forecasts or models involve the assumption that an exhaustive set of forecasts or models is being considered. If the set is non-exhaustive, as is usually the case, the proofs do not go through. Thus, whether it is "optimal" or "beneficial" to combine forecasts or models is still an open issue that unfortunately cannot be decided on logical grounds. Empirical analysis is needed to help settle the issue.

Recognizing this last combining fact, in a paper with Min, we presented new Bayesian methods for combining fixed parameter and time-varying parameter models. After some laborious efforts, we finally managed to obtain computable Bayesian posterior odds relating to fixed parameter and time-varying, random parameter (RP) models, e.g. a model with a coefficient vector generated by a vector random walk process. That is, we started one to one on the FP model versus the RP model and then used the data to evaluate the posterior odds on the two models – say, 1.5 to 1 in favor of the RP model. The odds were employed, year by year, to choose between or among alternative models and their forecasts. Also, using my earlier results on deriving an optimal combining density as one that is closest in an information theoretic sense to the individual densities being considered, we derived optimal combining predictive densities, updated them year by year, and used their associated predictive means as point forecasts. Such predictive means are optimal forecasts relative to a quadratic predictive loss function. In calculations with data for eighteen countries, we compared the forecasting performance of combined models with that of individual models. In our experiments, we found that combining forecasts in this instance led to small improvements in forecasting performance. Further, it was established that the Bayesian forecast combining techniques worked better than non-Bayesian forecast combining techniques.

In a published review of our paper by R. Fildes, an editor of the *International Journal of Forecasting*, he wrote in 1994 (pp. 163–164) that the alternative models and methods

> were carefully compared based on their individual country performance measured by root mean squared error for the years 1974–1987, and the distribution of these (particularly the median).

The results offer mild support for using time-varying parameter schemes. Pooling is important in improving accuracy. Model selection schemes are not particularly helpful except in so far as they identify pooled TVP (time-varying parameter) models as the most accurate forecasting models. Combining does not improve over the TVP models and, with the Granger-Ramanathan unconstrained scheme for choosing the weights, led to substantially poorer accuracy. Equal weights were not considered. This paper is an excellent example of good empirical economics where the theory is utilized effectively in analyzing the problem in hand.[74]

1.9   Turning point forecasting methods and results

While point forecasting work gave us some important evidence regarding the forecasting performance of our basic ARLI model and variants of it, a much more demanding test involves the ability to forecast cyclical downturns and upturns in economic activity accurately. As mentioned earlier, in our past work and in work by others, it has been found that time series models, e.g. random walk, AR(3), ARIMA and others, perform poorly in forecasting turning points. The same can be said of many macroeconometric models.

In approaching this problem, it is necessary to define what is meant by a "downturn" (DT) or "no downturn" (NDT) and by an "upturn" (UT) or "no upturn" (NUT), as recognized earlier by William Wecker and John Kling.[75] Among many possible definitions, we settled on the following simple definitions regarding the behavior of annual rates of growth of real GDP. Given that we are in year T, with growth rate y(T), and have observed two previous growth rates, $y(T-2)$ and $y(T-1)$, if the previous growth rates and next year's, as yet unobserved growth rate, $y(T+1)$, satisfy the following relation, we state that a DT has occurred in year $T+1$:

$$y(T-2), y(T-1) < y(T) > y(T+1) \quad \text{DT in year } T+1$$

$$(1.8)$$

Also, if the data and the as yet unobserved growth rate for period T + 1 satisfy the following relation, an NDT event has occurred:

$$y(T-2), y(T-1) < y(T) < y(T+1) \quad \text{NDT in year } T+1$$

(1.9)

Similarly, for UT and NUT events in year T + 1, we have for the definition of an UT:

$$y(T-2), y(T-1) > y(T) < y(T+1) \quad \text{UT in year } T+1$$

(1.10)

and:

$$y(T-2), y(T-1) > y(T) > y(T+1) \quad \text{NUT in year } T+1$$

(1.11)

Thus, if we have two successive growth rates below the third and the fourth is below the third, we have a DT, while, if the fourth is not below the third, there is NDT. Also, if we have two successive growth rates above the third and if the fourth is above the third, we have an UT, while, if the fourth is not above the third, we have a NUT.

While these are not the only definitions that can be employed, they are operational and easily comprehensible. Assuming that two previous growth rates are below the current growth rate and given data up to period T, D_T, the Bayesian predictive density for $y(T+1)$ associated with one of our models is readily available. See figure 1.2 for a plot of this predictive density. Using this predictive density, it is easy to compute the probability that next year's rate of growth, $y(T+1)$, will be less than this year's rate of growth – that is, the probability of a DT, namely $\Pr(DT) = \Pr(Y(T+1) < Y(T) \mid D)$, where D stands for past prior and sample information and the condition defining a DT/NDT episode. Also, the probability of NDT is $\Pr(NDT) = \Pr(Y(T+1) > Y(T) \mid D) = 1 - \Pr(DT)$. See figure 1.2 for a graphic representation of $\Pr(DT)$ and $\Pr(NDT)$.

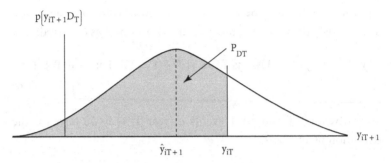

Figure 1.2 Calculation of probability of a downturn in period $T + 1$

Given that we have computed the values of $\Pr(DT)$ and $\Pr(NDT)$, we can use these probabilities in association with a 2×2 loss structure to determine an optimal turning point forecast – namely the one of the two possible forecasts that has lower expected loss associated with it. Explicitly in terms of the loss structure, shown in figure 1.3, expected loss associated with the choice of a DT forecast is $a\Pr(NDT)$ while that associated with an NDT forecast is $b\Pr(DT)$. On comparing these expected losses, we choose the forecast with the smaller expected loss. That is, if $a\Pr(NDT) < b\Pr(DT)$, we choose the forecast DT, while, if the inequality is reversed, we choose the NDT forecast. In the special case of a symmetric loss structure, $a = b$, we shall choose the DT forecast if $\Pr(NDT) = 1 - \Pr(DT) < \Pr(DT)$; that is, if $\Pr(DT) > \frac{1}{2}$. Similarly, if the $\Pr(NDT) > \frac{1}{2}$ or, equivalently, $\Pr(DT) < \frac{1}{2}$, we choose the DT forecast.

An analysis similar to that shown above can be employed to derive optimal UT/NUT forecasts using the probability of an UT computed from a predictive density function. Again, an optimal turning point forecast, e.g. an UT, can be obtained using a 2×2 loss structure. If the loss structure is symmetric, the optimal turning point forecast is to forecast an UT if $\Pr(UT) > \frac{1}{2}$ and a NUT if $\Pr(UT) < \frac{1}{2}$.

Shown in table 1.4 are computed probabilities of downturns in the rates of growth in real GDP for eighteen countries in upper turning point episodes. It is clearly the case that the computed probabilities contain information regarding future movements of countries' growth

Loss structure

	Outcomes		Expected losses
	DT	NDT	
DT	0	a	aPr(NDT)
Forecasts			
NDT	b	0	bPr(DT)
Probabilities	Pr(DT)	Pr(NDT)	

Figure 1.3 Loss structure

Note: a and b are non-negative losses. Losses have been scaled so that zero losses are associated with correct forecasts.

rates. Probabilities relating to upturns are shown in table 1.5. Again, it is the case that the probabilities provide information about future movements.

When we forecast using the above "$\frac{1}{2}$ rule" – namely – forecasting a DT given that the Pr(DT) > $\frac{1}{2}$ and NDT otherwise – we see from figure 1.4 that, in 158 turning point forecasts for eighteen countries, 1974–86, use of a variety of our ARLI models, with and without pooling, led to more than 70 percent of the turning point forecasts being correct. In the case of the TVP/ARLI/WI model, with or without pooling, and the pooled EW/ARLI/WI (exponentially weighted) and FP/ARLI/WI models, the percentages of correct forecasts were about eighty. Similarly, as shown in figure 1.5, the percentages of seventy-six DT or NDT forecasts being correct were about seventy or higher for all the models considered, with results using pooling quite a bit better than those without use of pooling or shrinkage. As regards eighty-two UT or NUT forecasts, in figure 1.5 we see that about 70 percent were correct. The results (see table 1.6) seem to indicate that the DT/NDT forecasts were slightly better than the UT/NUT forecasts in terms of percentages of correct forecasts.

Table 1.4 *Computed probabilities of downturns by year and country from the pooled TVP/ARLI/WI model*[a]

Country	1974	1975	1976	1977	1978	1979	1980	1981	1982	1983	1984	1985	1986
Australia				0.68*			0.83*					0.94	
Austria	0.82*			0.77*			0.95*				0.27*	0.54*	0.36*
Belgium				0.90*				0.89*					
Canada	0.94*			0.91*							0.37–	0.88*	
Denmark				0.95*		0.13–	0.80*			0.65*		0.33–	0.36*
Finland							0.93*						0.69*
France	0.87*			0.88*						0.44*			0.51–
Germany				0.92*	0.74*		0.85*				0.27–	0.64*	
Ireland									0.92*			0.60*	
Italy	0.81*			0.87*	0.55*		0.81*					0.66*	
Japan				0.83–								0.67*	
Netherlands	0.88*			0.84*			0.70*				0.23–	0.58*	
Norway		0.98*		0.95*			0.78*				0.58–	0.66–	
Spain					0.51*		0.80*				0.44–	0.31–	0.37–
Sweden	0.68*					0.12–	0.80*	0.91*			0.37–	0.80*	
Switzerland					0.47*		0.74–			0.32–		0.57–	0.77*
United Kingdom	0.99*			0.85*		0.31*					0.54*		0.44*
United States	0.86*			0.85*		0.52*					0.42–	0.96*	

[a] An asterisk (*) indicates that a downturn occurred while a dash (–) indicates that a downturn did not occur.

Table 1.5 *Computed probabilities of upturns by year and country from the pooled TVP/ARLI/WI model*[a]

Country	Year												
	1974	1975	1976	1977	1978	1979	1980	1981	1982	1983	1984	1985	1986
Australia		0.11*			0.45*			0.77*		0.31*			
Austria	0.42–	0.12–	0.90*			0.92*			0.57*				
Belgium		0.04–	0.96*						0.74*				
Canada		0.05–	0.77*					0.56*		0.95*			
Denmark		0.25*				0.86*		0.80–	0.95*				
Finland		0.20–	0.89–	0.51*					0.71*				
France	0.39–	0.19–	0.89*					0.41–	0.55*		0.90*		
Germany		0.70–	0.98*					0.61–	0.64–	0.80*			
Ireland		0.04–	0.67–	0.73*			0.34*			0.15–	0.98*		
Italy			0.96*						0.53–	0.42*			
Japan		0.05*						0.12–	0.48–	0.31*			
Netherlands			0.97*			0.74*		0.63–	0.70–	0.89*			
Norway	0.82*	0.09–	0.70*		0.38*			0.12–	0.63–	0.71*			
Spain					0.82*	0.79–	0.81*	0.69–	0.81*				
Sweden			0.54–	0.60–					0.82*				0.57–
Switzerland	0.30–	0.16–	0.99*						0.28–	0.89*			
United Kingdom		0.55*						0.80*					
United States		0.52–	0.90*				0.57–	0.76*		0.91*			0.80*

[a] An asterisk (*) indicates that an upturn occurred while a dash (–) indicates that an upturn did not occur. See eq. (1.7) in the text for the definition.

Percentages of correct forecasts

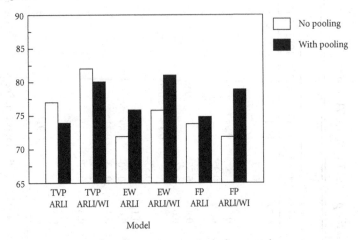

Figure 1.4 Percentages of turning points correctly forecasted

This rather good turning point forecasting performance came as a pleasant surprise. However, it may be that some benchmark models could do as well. In this connection, the following "naïve" turning point forecasters were created. First, there is the "eternal optimist," who in an upper turning point episode, as defined above, always forecasts NDT. Similarly, our eternal optimist always forecasts UT in a lower turning point episode. Second, there is the "eternal pessimist," who always forecasts DT at the top and NUT at the bottom. Third, there is the "deterministic four-year cycle" forecaster, who always forecasts DT at the top and UT at the bottom. As shown in table 1.7 these "naïve" or "benchmark" forecasters do not do nearly as well as the ARLI-type models in forecasting turning points. For example, of 158 turning points, the eternal optimist gets just 41 percent correct. The eternal pessimist does a bit better in getting 59 percent correct, while the deterministic four-year cycle forecaster does the best with 68 percent correct. On the other hand, all the ARLI-type models had over 70 percent correct, with three having 80 percent or more correct. Similarly, with respect to DT/NDT and UT/NUT forecasts, the models performed better than the naïve turning point forecasters.

Percentages of correct DT/NDT forecasts

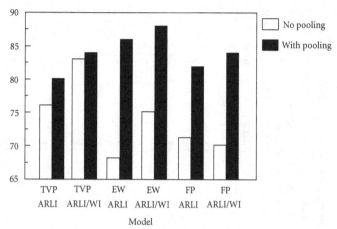

Percentages of correct UT/NUT forecasts

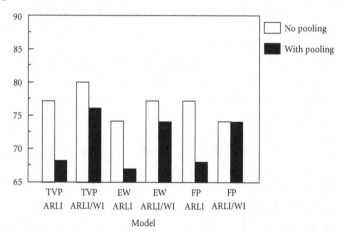

Figure 1.5 Percentages of correct downturn / no downturn and upturn / no upturn forecasts

Table 1.6 *Forecasting turning points in annual growth rates, eighteen countries, 1974–86, using various models*

Model	Percentage of correct forecasts			Number of incorrect forecasts		
	158 turning point forecasts	76 DT & NDT forecasts	82 UT & NUT forecasts	158 turning point forecasts	76 DT & NDT forecasts	82 UT & NUT forecasts
{A} *No pooling*						
1 TVP/ARLI	77	76	77	37	18	19
2 TVP/ARLI/WI	82	83	80	29	13	16
3 EW/ARLI	72	68	74	45	24	21
4 EW/ARLI/WI	76	75	77	38	19	19
5 FP/ARLI	74	71	77	41	22	19
6 FP/ARLI/WI	72	70	74	44	23	21
{B} *With pooling*						
7 TVP/ARLI	74	80	68	41	15	26
8 TVP/ARLI/WI	80	84	76	32	12	20
9 EW/ARLI	76	86	67	38	11	27
10 EW/ARLI/WI	81	88	74	30	9	21
11 FP/ARLI	75	82	68	40	14	26
12 FP/ARLI/WI	79	84	74	33	12	21

Table 1.7 *Performance of various procedures for forecasting turning points in annual output growth rates for eighteen countries, 1974–86*

Forecasting procedure	Number and percentage of incorrect forecasts[a]		
	76 DT/NDT forecasts	82 UT/NUT forecasts	158 turning point forecasts
1 Eternal[b] optimist	59 (78)	34 (41)	93 (59)
2 Eternal pessimist[c]	17 (22)	48 (59)	65 (41)
3 Deterministic four-year cycle[d]	17 (22)	34 (41)	51 (32)
4 TVP/ARLI/WI			
Unpooled	13 (17)	16 (20)	29 (18)
Pooled	12 (16)	20 (24)	32 (20)

[a] Figures in parentheses are percentages of incorrect forecasts.
[b] An eternal optimist forecasts either UT or NDT.
[c] An eternal pessimist forecasts either DT or NUT.
[d] Forecasts either DT or UT.

Another naïve turning point forecaster is a fair coin flipper. With 158 turning point episodes, a coin flipper would expect or forecast that $\frac{1}{2}(158) = 79$ actual DTs and UTs would occur. In the data there are 107 DTs and UTs out of 158 cases – quite a bit more than expected by the coin flipper. For each of our models and each turning point episode, the probabilities of each DT or of each UT were computed and added over the 158 turning point episodes to get the expected number of turning points, with results shown in table 1.8. It is seen that the expected numbers vary from 94 to 104, much closer to the actual number observed – 107, than provided by the coin flipping procedure, namely an expected number equal to 79.

The results of these turning point forecasting experiments were so pleasing that I decided to share them with Milton Friedman, a colleague and good friend. While he was pleasantly surprised by the

Table 1.8 *Expected number of turning points, downturns and upturns*

Model	Unpooled	Pooled
1 TVP/ARLI	104	98
2 TVP/ARLI/WI	101	98
3 EW/ARLI	101	102
4 EW/ARLI/WI	98	98
5 FP/ARLI	100	99
6 FP/ARLI/WI	96	94
Actual number of TPTs	107	107
Total number of cases	158	158

results, he suggested that we extend the sample to see whether our results would hold up using new data. Also, he pointed to a difference between experimental testing of procedures and on-line testing of procedures, where, among other things, one has to deal with the "preliminary data" problem. That is, preliminary estimates of, for example, GDP can differ considerably from revised estimates and also revisions take place not just once but quite a few times – as I found when I was completing my doctoral dissertation dealing with quarterly consumption and personal disposable income data. I found that revisions in the most recent data were very large and wrote an article on the topic after completing my dissertation, in which I described properties of revisions in a number of variables in our national income and product accounts.[76] There is no question but that good procedures are needed to deal with the "preliminary data revision problem" in connection with obtaining good forecasts. Recognizing this, it still seemed of great interest to determine how our turning point forecasting methods would perform on an expanded sample of data for our eighteen countries. Thus, data for the period 1974–95 were collected from the IMF database, and it was found that the expanded database included 211 turning point episodes, as defined above. On using the

ARLI-type models and turning point forecasting methods, described above, to analyze the new data set, again 70 percent or more of the turning point forecasts were correct – much better than the forecasting performance of our naïve turning point forecasters and our coin flipper.[77]

1.10   Compatibility with economic theory

Having obtained models that perform reasonably well in point and turning point forecasting, in the SEMTSA approach the next step is to determine the extent to which the models are compatible with economic theory. It was not too hard to develop an aggregate demand and supply model, from which it is possible algebraically to derive an equation for the rate of growth of real output that resembles our ARLI/WI model. Also, Chansik Hong, in his doctoral dissertation at the University of Chicago, derived our ARLI/WI model from a version of Hicks' IS/LM model, and Chung-ki Min in his doctoral dissertation formulated a generalized real business cycle model and showed that it implied a model similar to our ARLI/WI model.[78]

Thus the ARLI/WI model is compatible with certain well-known macroeconomic models that are featured in macroeconomic texts. While this is reassuring, in our continuing efforts to improve our models it was noted that many macroeconomic models do not allow adequately for the different cyclical and trend characteristics of industrial sectors – say, agriculture, construction, mining, etc. Further, in some real business cycle models there is a representative firm, and one wonders what happens if the representative firm shuts down. No allowance has been made for the entry and exit of firms – a very important aspect of business fluctuations. Also, note that in Muth's famous paper on rational expectations in a competitive industry he, and later many others, assumed a constant number of firms. On hearing of this assumption, Marshall probably turned over in his grave. Finally, there is the issue of the emergence of new industrial sectors – e.g. the computer industry, etc. – that are important in affecting growth

Table 1.9 *RMSEs and MAEs of one-year-ahead aggregate and disaggregate forecasts of the median of eighteen countries' annual real GDP growth rates[a]*

A: 1974–84

	Disaggregate AR(3)LI[b] with $\hat{w}_t$ eqn. (1.6)	Disaggregate AR(3)LI for w_t eqn. (1.4)	Disaggregate AR(3)LI eqn. (1.5)
RMSE	1.30	1.60	1.66
MAE	1.21	1.43	1.44

B: 1980–95

	Disaggregate AR(3)LI with $\gamma_i = \gamma$, $\delta_{ji} = \delta_j$ eqn. (1.5)	Disaggregate AR(3)LI for w_t eqn. (1.4)	Disaggregate AR(3)LI with $\delta_{ji} = \delta_j$, $j = 4, 5, 6, 7$ eqn. (1.5)	Disaggregate AR(3)LI eqn. (1.5)
RMSE	1.61	1.60	1.76	1.84
MAE	1.35	1.42	1.46	1.56

	Disaggregate AR(3)LI with $\hat{w}_t$ $\phi_i = \phi, \gamma_i = \gamma, \delta_{ji} = \delta_j$ eqn. (1.6)	Disaggregate AR(3)LI with $\hat{w}_t$ $\phi_i = \phi, \delta_{ji} = \delta_j, j = 4, 5, 6, 7$ eqn. (1.6)	Disaggregate AR(3)LI with $\hat{w}_t$ eqn. (1.6)
RMSE	1.42	1.46	1.52
MAE	1.25	1.28	1.35

[a] The data are taken from the IMF computerized database at the University of Chicago. We use data for the following eighteen countries: Australia, Austria, Belgium, Canada, Denmark, Finland, France, Germany, Ireland, Italy, Japan, the Netherlands, Norway, Spain, Sweden, Switzerland, the United Kingdom and the United States. Observations are available from 1954 to 1995 for most countries (with some countries' data dating back to 1948), but begin in 1971 for Germany. Omitting Germany from the analysis produces similar results. We define $\mathrm{RMSE} = \sqrt{\sum_{t=t}^{T}(\hat{w}_t - w_t)^2 T}$, and similarly $\mathrm{MAE} = (\sum_{t=t}^{T} |\hat{w}_t - w_t|)/T$.
[b] AR(3)LI denotes an autoregressive model of order three containing leading indicator variables. See, e.g., equation (1.4) in the text.

and fluctuations in output and other variables, as Schumpeter, Hansen, Gordon and many others have recognized.

1.11   The Marshallian macroeconomic model

With the above considerations in mind, it occurred to me that an MMM would be worthwhile to consider and might yield improved explanatory and predictive performance. By considering various sectors of an economy, many more observations would be available on sector-specific variables as well as on aggregate variables. Also, specific features of sectors – say, agriculture, construction, mining, etc. – could be modeled and might improve explanatory and predictive performance. Of course, the argument that disaggregation might yield improved modeling results had been forcefully presented by Guy Orcutt for many years.[79] And, indeed, some macroeconometric modelers did disaggregate in various ways, including Stone, the Leontieff input-outputters, the FRB-MIT-PENN macroeconometric modelers and others.

To show that disaggegation could lead to improved forecasts, equation (1.7) was employed to forecast the median growth of eighteen countries' growth rates of real GDP – an aggregative approach. As an alternative, equations (1.6) and (1.7) were employed to obtain annual growth rate forecasts for each of the eighteen countries, and the median of the eighteen countries' annual forecasts was used as a forecast. As shown in table 1.9, the second, disaggregative procedure produced much better annual forecasts, indicating that, in this instance, it paid to disaggregate.[80] Also, there were analytical results indicating that working with disaggregated data could lead to improved forecasts of aggregate variables.[81] Of course, if models for the disaggregated data and the disaggregated data are of poor quality, then obviously there may be no advantages associated with disaggregation. On the other hand, with good disaggregated data and appropriate models for them, better forecasts of aggregate data may be obtained. In addition, obviously, forecasts of disaggregated sector variables are available.

With the above considerations in mind, the problem of how to dis-aggregate arose. It was possible to go all the way to models with an extremely detailed level of disaggregation, e.g. Leontieff input-output models or Orcutt micro-simulation models. While these possibilities were considered, it was thought more advisable to approach the disaggregation process step by step. A first step was to adopt a Marshallian sector view of the economy, with each sector having demand, supply *and* entry equations; a sophisticatedly simple model that has been shown to be useful in many different contexts over the years. As noted above, most macroeconomic models have not considered entry and exit of firms at all. Note that, in the 1930s Depression in the United States, about 20 percent of the firms industry by industry shut down with an enormous impact on supply. Also, the primary mechanism producing long-run equilibrium in a Marshallian industry model is the entry and exit of firms.

With these considerations in mind, it was decided to formulate simple competitive Marshallian models of eleven sectors of the US economy, using annual data in an effort to investigate the extent to which disaggregation might help in improving forecasts of aggregate variables and their growth rates, e.g. total real US GDP and its growth rate, obtained by adding sector GDP forecasts to get a forecast of the total each year. In a working paper, de Alba and I had shown that, under a variety of conditions, improved forecasts could be obtained, given that sectors' input variables were not identical or highly positively correlated, and, obviously, if the sector models and data were adequate.[82]

In our work to construct an MMM, we assumed individual firms in a sector to be operating with Cobb-Douglas production functions incorporating neutral and factor-augmenting technological change (an elaboration of a production function used in an earlier study of the Canadian furniture industry), and to be maximizing profits given product price and the prices of factor inputs, labor and capital.[83] From the profit-maximizing solution, we derived the supply function for an individual firm and the industry supply function, which involved the number of firms in operation in year t, denoted by $N(t)$. By multiplying the individual firm's supply function by $N(t)$ and $p(t)$, the real price of output, we obtained the sector's real sales function in year t, $S(t)$, which depends on: $N(t)$, the number of firms in operation; $p(t)$, the real price of output; technological change, $A(t)$ – the product of neutral and factor-augmenting technical change; and the real prices of factor inputs, labor, capital, etc. Along with this supply function, we introduced a demand equation for the sector's output and an entry equation. When the three equations were solved for the implied relation for industry real sales, $S(t)$, in the continuous time version of the model, the differential equation for $S(t)$ assumed the following form:

$$(1/S)dS/dt = a(1 - S/F) + g \qquad (1.12)$$

where a and F are positive parameters and $g = g(t)$ is a linear function of the rates of change of variables shifting demand and supply relations, e.g. real income, real money balances, real wage, real price of capital, etc.

If in equation (1.12) $g = 0$ or $g = $ constant, the solution to the differential equation is the well-known "S-shaped" logistic function with $(1 + g/a)F$, the long-run equilibrium value of real sales. Also, when a sector is in long-run equilibrium, when g changes – perhaps due to a change in a demand shifter, e.g. real income, or a supply shifter, e.g. the real wage rate – the sector growth rate is disturbed from its equilibrium value and a movement to restore a new equilibrium through the entry or exit of firms is initiated. Also, it should be noted that, if there is a discrete lag in equation (1.12), it is in the form of a mixed differential-difference equation model, and the movement to the new equilibrium can involve oscillatory features. In a sense, this model with a discrete lag provides a "structural" Marshallian rationalization of the well-known Friedman "plucking model" of the business cycle. Further, as a former student, Mervin Daub, recently suggested, it is possible to add the sectors' equilibrium values of S to obtain a new, operational definition of full employment real GDP. Last, as has been recognized in a recent paper, the discrete version of equation (1.12) is in the form of a canonical "chaotic model" solution, which can exhibit a wide range of rather interesting and unusual oscillatory and non-oscillatory properties.[84]

In figure 1.6, annual data for real GDP relating to eleven sectors of the US economy between 1949 and 1997 are plotted. It is seen that the sectors' data exhibit very different characteristics, with the agriculture, mining, durable and construction sectors showing much greater variability than other sectors; see the box plots of the sector growth rates in figure 1.7, which graphically display the differences in sector output growth rate variability. As emphasized in the early business cycle literature, interaction between or among sectors is an important element in understanding why some downturns are so severe and others are relatively mild. Thus, there appears to be additional information in the disaggregated sector models that may be helpful in improving forecasts of aggregate variables.

In recent work with B. Chen, published in *Macroeconomic Dynamics*, various discrete time series models approximating equation (1.12) have been formulated (see table 1.10) and fitted using annual real GDP data for eleven sectors of the US economy 1949–79, and then used to calculate one-year-ahead forecasts of sectors' real GDP, which were added to provide a forecast of total real GDP and its growth rate.[85] When these "disaggregate" forecasts were compared with forecasts of total US real GDP derived from AR(3) and other time series models implemented with aggregate data, it was found that use of the sector model and disaggregate data led to considerable improvement in forecast accuracy. For example, from table 1.11, we see that, when an AR(3) model was used to forecast annual US real GDP growth rates 1980–97, with parameter estimates updated year by year, the RMSE of forecast was 2.32 percentage points while the mean absolute error (MAE) of forecast was 1.71 percentage points. Also, this AR(3) model missed all the turning points. While ARLI and an ARLI model with

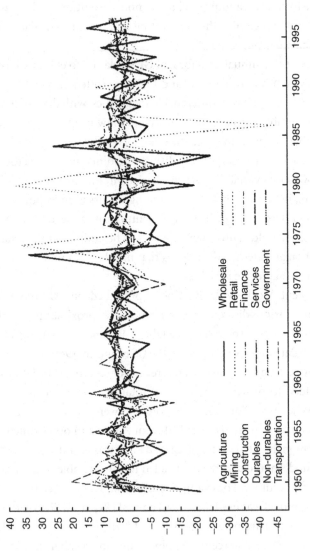

Figure 1.6 US sectoral real output growth rates

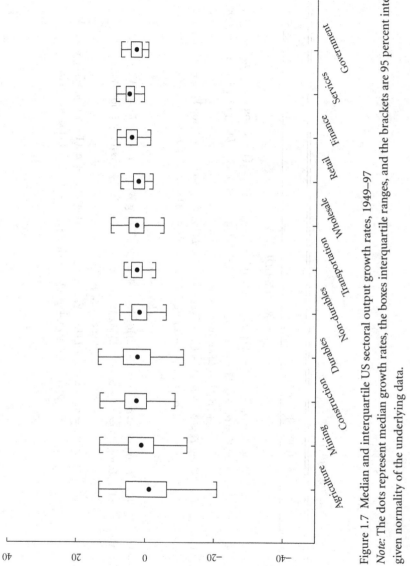

Figure 1.7 Median and interquartile US sectoral output growth rates, 1949–97

Note: The dots represent median growth rates, the boxes interquartile ranges, and the brackets are 95 percent intervals given normality of the underlying data.

Table 1.10 *Forecasting equations*[a]

Model	Reduced from equations

Real US GDP

AR(3)(A): $(1-L)\log Y_t = \alpha_0 + \alpha_1(1-L)\log Y_{t-1} + \alpha_2(1-L)\log Y_{t-2} + \alpha_3(1-L)\log Y_{t-3} + u_t$

AR(3)LI(A): $(1-L)\log Y_t = \alpha_0 + \alpha_1(1-L)\log Y_{t-1} + \alpha_2(1-L)\log Y_{t-2} + \alpha_3(1-L)\log Y_{t-3} + \beta_1(1-L)\log SR_{t-1}$
$\qquad + \beta_2(1-L)\log m_{t-1} + u_t$

MMM(A): $(1-L)\log Y_t = \alpha_0 + \alpha_1(1-L)\log Y_{t-1} + \alpha_2(1-L)\log Y_{t-2} + \alpha_3(1-L)\log Y_{t-3} + \alpha_4\,Y_{t-1} + \alpha_5\,Y_{t-2}$
$\qquad + \alpha_6\,t + \beta_1(1-L)\log SR_{t-1} + \beta_2(1-L)\log m_{t-1} + u_t$

Real Wage

AR(3) (A): $(1-L)\log W_t = \alpha_0 + \alpha_1(1-L)\log W_{t-1} + \alpha_2(1-L)\log W_{t-2} + \alpha_3(1-L)\log W_{t-3} + u_t$

AR(3)LI(A): $(1-L)\log W_t = \alpha_0 + \alpha_1(1-L)\log W_{t-1} + \alpha_2(1-L)\log W_{t-2} + \alpha_3(1-L)\log W_{t-3}$
$\qquad + \beta_1(1-L)\log SR_{t-1} + \beta_2(1-L)\log m_{t-1} + u_t$

MMM(A): $(1-L)\log W_t = \alpha_0 + \alpha_1(1-L)\log W_{t-1} + \alpha_2(1-L)\log W_{t-2} + \alpha_3(1-L)\log W_{t-3} + \gamma_1\,W_{t-1}$
$\qquad + \gamma_2\,W_{t-2} + \gamma_3\,t + \beta_1(1-L)\log SR_{t-1} + \beta_2(1-L)\log m_{t-1} + u_t$

Model	Sectoral forecast equations
AR(3)(DA):	$(1 - L) \log S_t = \alpha_0 + \alpha_1(1 - L) \log S_{t-1} + \alpha_2(1 - L) \log S_{t-2} + \alpha_3(1 - L) \log S_{t-3} + u_t$
AR(3)LI(DA):	$(1 - L) \log S_t = \alpha_0 + \alpha_1(1 - L) \log S_{t-1} + \alpha_2(1 - L) \log S_{t-2} + \alpha_3(1 - L) \log S_{t-3} + \beta_1(1 - L) \log SR_{t-1}$ $\quad + \beta_2(1 - L) \log m_{t-1} + \beta_3(1 - L) \log W_t + \beta_4(1 - L) \log Y_t + u_t$
Distrib. Lag(DA):	$(1 - L) \log S_t = \alpha_0 + \alpha_1(1 - L) \log S_{t-1} + \beta_1(1 - L) \log SR_{t-1} + \beta_2(1 - L) \log m_{t-1} + \beta_3(1 - L) \log W_t$ $\quad + \beta_4(1 - L) \log Y_t + \beta_5(1 - L) \log W_{t-1} + \beta_6(1 - L) \log Y_{t-1} + u_t$
MMM(DA)I:	$(1 - L) \log S_t = \alpha_0 + \alpha_1 S_{t-1} + \beta_1(1 - L) \log SR_{t-1} + \beta_2(1 - L) \log m_{t-1} + \beta_3(1 - L) \log W_t$ $\quad + \beta_4(1 - L) \log Y_t + u_t$
MMM(DA)II:	$(1 - L) \log S_t = \alpha_0 + \alpha_1 S_{t-1} + \alpha_2 S_{t-2} + \beta_1(1 - L) \log SR_{t-1} + \beta_2(1 - L) \log m_{t-1} + \beta_3(1 - L) \log W_t$ $\quad + \beta_4(1 - L) \log Y_t + u_t$
MMM(DA)III:	$(1 - L) \log S_t = \alpha_0 + \alpha_1 S_{t-1} + \alpha_2 S_{t-2} + \alpha_3 S_{t-3} + \beta_1(1 - L) \log SR_{t-1} + \beta_2(1 - L) \log m_{t-1}$ $\quad + \beta_3(1 - L) \log W_t + \beta_4(1 - L) \log Y_t + u_t$
MMM(AD)IV:	$(1 - L) \log S_t = \alpha_0 + \alpha_1 S_{t-1} + \alpha_2 S_{t-1} + \beta_1(1 - L) \log SR_{t-1} + \beta_2(1 - L) \log m_{t-1} + \beta_3(1 - L) \log W_t$ $\quad + \beta_4(1 - L) \log Y_t + u_t$

[a] In equation descriptions, (A) denotes aggregate and (DA) denotes disaggregate.

Table 1.11 *RMSEs for pooled and unpooled ARLI/WI models' forecasts by country, 1974–87*

RMSE (%)	Countries	Freq.	Prop.
	A. Pooled TVP model		
1.00–1.49	FRN GER NET SPN	4	0.22
1.50–1.99	AUR BEL CAN FIN ITY NOR SWD UKM USA	9	0.50
2.00–2.99	AUL DEN JAP SWZ	4	0.22
2.50–2.99	IRE	1	0.06
3.00–3.49	—	0	0.00
	Median = 1.74 Minimum = 1.17 Maximum = 2.53	18	1.00
	B. Unpooled TVP model		
1.00–1.49	UKM	1	0.06
1.50–1.99	BEL FRN GER NET SPN SWD	6	0.33
2.00–2.49	AUR USA	2	0.11
2.50–2.99	CAN DEN ITY NOR	4	0.22
3.00–3.49	AUL FIN IRE JAP SWZ	5	0.28
	Median = 2.37 Minimum = 1.39 Maximum = 3.32	18	1.00
	C. Pooled FP model		
1.00–1.49	NOR SPN	2	0.11
1.50–1.99	AUR BEL CAN FIN FRN GER NET SWD UKM	9	0.50
2.00–2.49	AUL DEN IRE ITY JAP SWZ USA	7	0.39
2.50–2.99	—	0	0.00
3.00–3.49	—	0	0.00
	Median = 1.86 Minimum = 1.21 Maximum = 2.48	18	1.00
	D. Unpooled FP model		
1.00–1.49	—	0	0.00
1.50–1.99	BEL NET NOR UKM USA	5	0.28
2.00–2.49	FRN SPN SWD	3	0.17
2.50–2.99	AUR CAN GER IRE	4	0.22
3.00–3.49	AUL DEN FIN JAP SWZ	5	0.28
3.50–3.99	ITY	1	0.06
	Median = 2.60 Minimum = 1.50 Maximum = 3.68	18	1.01

lagged levels of real GDP and a trend variable included performed better than the AR(3) model, they did not perform as well as the forecasts derived by adding sector forecasts of real GDP to get a forecast of total GDP and its growth rate, with year-by-year updating of sector models' parameter estimates. See figure 1.8 for plots of actual and forecasted values year by year. Variants of these "disaggregate" MMM forecasts had RMSEs ranging from 1.40 percentage points to 1.92 percentage points and MAEs ranging from 1.17 percentage points to 1.62 percentage points. The lowest MAE, of 1.17 percentage points, was encountered when the set of sector equations was treated as a seemingly unrelated regression system and estimated taking account of sector error terms, differing error term variances and error term correlations. However, in many instances, other Bayesian and non-Bayesian estimation procedures, some allowing for possible endogeneity of input variables – e.g. real income and the real wage rate – produced rather good results. However, disaggregate forecasts derived from AR(3) models fitted with sector data did not show much, if any, improvement relative to an AR(3) model implemented with the aggregate data.

Thus, these forecasting experiments indicate that our "first approximation" sector Marshallian macroeconomic modeling approach appears to be promising. However, the models for several sectors, particularly agriculture, mining and construction, need improvement. Also, perhaps allowing for departures from competitive conditions, using more elaborate entry equation formulations, allowing for discreteness in demand for durables, using more input variables, fitting sector equations jointly rather than just one equation per sector, etc. can lead to improved forecasts. Also, if good quarterly data are available by sector, models using them may lead to more improvement in explanatory and forecasting performance, particularly if variables' seasonal variation and seasonal components' interaction with cyclical and trend components are carefully modeled. Last, by adding markets for factors, e.g. labor, money, capital, a government sector and an export sector, we have a complete macroeconomic model that

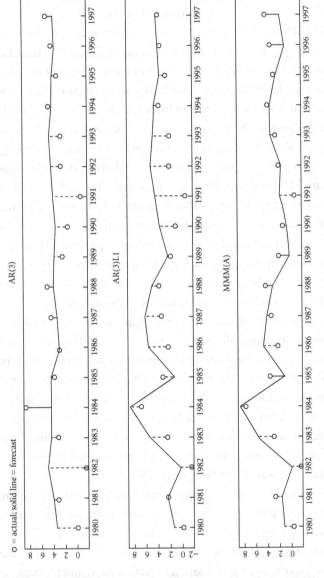

Figure 1.8 Actual and forecasted values

permits a broader range of variables to be forecasted and problems to be analyzed.

Implementation of our SEMTSA approach has been rewarding in terms of producing models that are operational with reasonably good performance in point and turning point forecasting experiments. Fortunately, not only were statistical time series models produced, but also these models have been rationalized using macroeconomic theory. Further, the philosophy to start simply and complicate only if necessary has led to the discovery of the MMM, a sector-based model that accommodates demand, supply and entry considerations as well as the birth of new sectors and the death of old sectors, à la Schumpeter and recently considered endogenous growth models. Theoretically and practically, use of these models is satisfying in terms of their explanatory power and their direct, practical forecasting and policy analysis uses. E.g., in evaluating the effects of a change in real money on demand, account can be taken of the differential real balance effects on durable goods and services as compared to those on non-durable goods.[86] Similarly, different effects of tax cuts on demand in different sectors can be utilized, thereby avoiding aggregation effects that, as is well known, can afflict estimates derived from aggregate data with serious biases. Further, use of time-varying parameter models or state equation systems, as the engineers call them, can take account of changes in parameter values over time in response to changes in tastes, technology, policies, etc., and appear to be favored over fixed parameter models by calculated posterior odds based on past data in our work with ARLI models using aggregate data. Possibly, use of an MMM with time-varying parameters and Bayesian shrinkage may provide improved results, as was the case with Quintana, Chopra and Putnam in their forecasting of international exchange rates[87].

Last, but not least, the integration of micro- and macroeconomics is a distinguishing feature of our Marshallian macroeconomic model. Departures from competitive conditions in certain sectors can be modeled and effects on an economy's performance determined, analytically or in simulation studies. Similarly, alternative governmental policies' effects can be evaluated analytically or in simulation experiments.

As our research on statistics, econometrics and forecasting continues in the years ahead, it will be a pleasure to share our results with the research staff of the Bank of England and other researchers. Hopefully, after many years of work by Richard Stone and many others, improved Bayesian statistical and econometric techniques can be combined with fruitful SEMTSA modeling techniques to provide us with sophisticatedly simple Marshallian macroeconomic models that explain the past and perform well in prediction and policy-making.

2

National Institute of Economic and Social Research

MAY 9, 2001

The National Institute of Economic and Social Research is an independent educational charity, founded in 1938. It conducts research on a wide variety of topics, but has a particular interest in economic modeling, investment and productivity, labour market issues and vocational education and training. All research projects are designed to contribute to the public debate on the issues they address. The Institute has its own research staff based in central London, and works in cooperation with universities, industry and other bodies. It is independent of UK government and receives no core funding from public or private sources.

The Institute aims to promote, through quantitative research, a deeper understanding of the interaction of economic and social forces that affect people's lives, in order that they may be improved. Its main function is to produce research suitable for publication through academic channels, and hence findings from the Institute's work are published widely in academic journals and elsewhere. They often find an outlet in the Institute's own quarterly *Economic Review*, which is available on subscription or individually. Discussion Papers dealing with work in progress, and Occasional Papers on specific topics, are also issued from time to time. Results from major pieces of research often lead to books, published through commercial publishers. In addition, the NIESR holds conferences each year, which provide an opportunity to hear about research findings and debate them with interested organisations and individuals.

National Institute of Economic and Social Research
2 Dean Trench Street, London SW1P 3HE
Tel: 020 7222 7665 Fax: 020 7654 1900

I am happy to be at the National Institute of Economic and Social Research to present the second Sir Richard Stone Lecture, a continuation of the discussion of statistics, econometrics and forecasting that I presented at the Bank of England several days ago. There I mentioned the debt that we owed to Sir Richard for his basic, fundamental contributions to both theoretical and applied statistics and econometrics, particularly his fruitful, practical and philosophical approach to research problems. See, for example, his classic 1954 book for an outstanding example of his influential research. Also, I pointed out at the Bank of England that a paradigm shift is taking place in theoretical and applied statistics and econometrics, namely a movement to a Bayesian approach to estimation, testing, prediction and decision-making procedures, in view of not only its strong philosophical basis but also, very importantly, its success in practical applications in many fields of science and application, including forecasting. With respect to the very difficult problem of the formulation of models that work well in explanation, prediction and policy-making, I described the SEMTSA approach that my colleagues and I have been pursuing in our work to produce good, structural macroeconometric models, and how it has led us to construct and test a multi-sector MMM.[1] Before going into detail about this model, I shall begin with some material relating to the general SEMTSA approach. Then I shall describe the implementation of it and end with theoretical and empirical analyses, including some forecasting results for our recently developed Marshallian macroeconomic model and possible extensions of it.

2.1 The structural econometric modeling, time series analysis (SEMTSA) approach

The SEMTSA approach to model building in statistics and econometrics originated years ago after I became familiar with the Box-Jenkins ARIMA modeling approach. George Box was a colleague in the Department of Statistics at the University of Wisconsin in Madison when I was a member of Wisconsin's Department of Economics during the early 1960s. Indeed, he played a major role in developing the Statistics Department with its many connections with other units of the university, including economics, business, engineering, computing, etc. It was indeed a case of British empire building at its best, which had many fruitful effects on research and teaching. In the 1960s, Box addressed the Econometrics Research Seminar on his current research with Gwilym Jenkins on ARIMA models, which led to their famous time series book. Earlier, I had reviewed Quenouille's excellent 1957 book on multiple time series models, including multivariate autoregressive moving average (MVARMA) models, and wondered how this time series work related to dynamic econometric simultaneous equations models of the sort that Tinbergen, Stone, Klein and many others constructed.[2] As usual, when I have a difficult problem, I formulate a simple variant of the complicated problem and try to solve it. If successful, I go on to other variants of the problem and sequentially approach the general solution. In this instance, I wondered whether it was possible to solve Quenouille's general model for the implied processes on individual variables and what form they would take. Also, I wondered how Quenouille's general MVARMA model was algebraically related to the class of dynamic simultaneous econometric models.

Having formulated the above two specific problems, fortunately it was not too hard to get answers, which were published in the 1970s in two articles co-authored by Franz Palm, who visited the University of Chicago for a couple of years as a graduate student and finished his doctoral dissertation at the University of Louvain under my direction as his "promoter." It was a pleasure to be at his degree ceremony, dressed up, along with other faculty members, in robes and hats that made us appear to be members of the Inquisition questioning the candidate. Fortunately, he answered all questions exceptionally well, to the pleasure of his parents and other friends who were present at the ceremony, and has since had a very productive career and wonderful family. I've often wondered how his very substantial output in research and teaching is measured in the national income and product accounts. My guess is that his, and others', considerable output in research and teaching is grossly underestimated in the national accounts; a topic that deserves much more attention, in my opinion. In fact, in correspondence with a former doctoral student of mine, Dr Brent Moulton, who recently was deeply involved in correcting price indices for quality change and in revising the US national income and product data, he told me that a revision of the data on the output and productivity of higher education was high on his list of items "to do" at the Bureau of Economic Analysis in Washington, DC. I also hope that he devises much-needed improved methods for measuring the output and productivity of government sectors worldwide, particularly in view of the huge amount of resources devoted to these sectors in most countries of the world. Measuring output of government sectors by factor inputs can produce very crude, biased measures, as is well known.

As regards the first of the two problems, mentioned above, the Quenouille multiple time series model, in the form of a MVARMA process, for an mx1 vector of variables, z(t), can be expressed as:

$$H(L)z(t) = F(L)e(t) \quad t = 1, 2, \ldots, T \quad (2.1)$$

where L is the lag operator such that $L^i z(t) = z(t-i)$ and $H(L)$ is an mxm matrix lag operator of degree p, i.e. $H(L) = I + H_1 L + H_2 L^2 + \cdots + H_p L^p$ where the H_i, $i = 1, 2, \ldots, p$, are mxm matrices with constant elements. Further, $F(L) = F_0 + F_1 L + F_2 L^2 \cdots + F_q L^q$ is an mxm matrix lag operator of degree q, with the F's mxm matrices with constant elements. The mx1 error vector $e(t)$ in equation (2.1) is assumed to have zero mean and to be serially uncorrelated – that is $Ee(t)e(t)' = 0$ for $t \neq t'$ and $= I$ for $t = t'$. Note that, if F is of degree zero – that is, $F(L) = F_0$ – equation (2.1) is a vector autoregression or, as I call it, a "very awful regression," for reasons to be explained below. Note too that, in the recent literature, there have been some misunderstandings about our system in equation (2.1) and its breadth of coverage. In writing the system, we do not necessarily assume stationarity nor do we always assume that the variables are always differenced to induce stationarity. In our interpretation of Quenouille's model, it is broad enough to accommodate variables in differenced form and/or level form, and thus we are not guilty of the charge leveled at us that the system in equation (2.1) is not broad enough to represent many multivariate linear time series models in use.[3] However, it does not represent the class of time-varying parameter models.

With respect to the first problem posed above, namely what the implied marginal processes are for individual elements of $z(t)$ – say the rate of change of real GDP – if $H(L)$ is invertible we have $z(t) = H^{-1} Fe(t) = (H_a/|H|) Fe(t)$, where $H^{-1} = H_a/|H|$, where $H_a = $ adjoint matrix associated with H, and the dependence of H and F on L is suppressed. Thus, the answer is:

$$|H|z(t) = H_a F e(t) \tag{2.2a}$$

or:

$$|H|z_{it} = a'_i e(t) \tag{2.2b}$$

where d_i is the ith row of $H_a F$. Since $|H|$ is usually a very high degree polynomial in the lag operator L, the process for z_{it} in equation (2.2b) is a high-order autoregression. Further, since the error term in (2.2b) is the sum of moving average processes for the individual elements of $e(t)$, under well-known conditions, it can be represented as a moving average process in terms of a single white noise error – say, $a_i(t)$. Thus, not only is the process for z_{it} in the Box-Jenkins ARMA form but, if there is no canceling of roots, the autoregressive process for each element of $z(t)$ will be of the same, usually high order with the same parameters. This result also holds for the special case of a VAR, where it is assumed that $F(L)$ is of degree zero – that is, $F(L) = F_0$ – and which has come to be known as the "autoregression paradox" since most empirical, statistical time series workers, using Box-Jenkins and other procedures, find low-order autoregressions for individual variables in empirical analyses and low-order moving average processes for individual variables using first differenced variables. Since such high-order autoregressive processes with identical autoregressive parameters are not observed in empirical time series analyses, this leads me to believe that unrestricted MVARMA or VAR processes are not generating the data that we observe.

Also, on considering the VARs used by Litterman and others in the 1980s, which had m = 7 and elements of $H(L)$ of sixth degree, the equation for each variable of the system in (2.1) has a dependent variable and $6 \times 7 = 42$ lagged input variables plus an intercept. Individually, it's like a regression with forty-two highly correlated input variables and an intercept term. With twenty years of quarterly data there are just eighty observations to fit a model with forty-three parameters, with the result that parameter estimates are not very precise, and, as Litterman discovered, the fitted – or "overfitted" – equations did not perform well in forecasting. While his use of a clever prior distribution for the parameters acted effectively to reduce the number of parameters somewhat and did result in improved forecasting performance for real variables, its performance for the financial variables was not satisfactory, as noted by Stephen McNees. Further, when Litterman's BVAR was employed by Christopher Sims and others at the Federal Reserve Bank of Minneapolis in the 1990s, it missed the 1990–91 downturn and was scheduled to be revised. Thus, whether Bayesian or non-Bayesian, VARs have not performed satisfactorily in forecasting, and this is one reason for my use of the term "very awful regressions." More fundamentally, the VAR, viewed by many as an encompassing model, is not a very sophisticatedly simple model, intuitively or more formally using Jeffreys' operational measure of the complexity of models applied to a VAR model. As equation (2.2b) indicates, it has strong implications that do not square with the information in the data. Thus, using it as an encompassing model, as some have done, is – in my opinion – a choice of the wrong model at the beginning, and testing downward will probably lead, unfortunately, to great disappointments. After all these years, as far as I know, such procedures have not as yet produced models that work well in explanation and prediction.

Now, to return to our second problem, namely how Quenouille's model in (2.1) relates to dynamic structural econometric models. Again, when the specific, direct question is formulated, it is not very hard to provide an answer after some thought. In the present case, the key difference between (2.1) and a dynamic simultaneous equations model is the fact that, in the latter, there are some variables – such as the weather etc. – that are assumed to be exogenously determined; that is, their variation is determined outside the dynamic simultaneous equations model. To accommodate such variables, the vector z_t is partitioned into $z'_t = (y'_t, x'_t)$, where y_t is a vector of endogenous variables and x_t is a vector of exogenous variables, and the system is written as follows with a partitioning of the $H(L)$ and $F(L)$ matrix lag operators:

$$\begin{pmatrix} H_{11} & H_{12} \\ H_{21} & H_{22} \end{pmatrix} \begin{pmatrix} y_t \\ x_t \end{pmatrix} = \begin{pmatrix} F_{11} & F_{12} \\ F_{21} & F_{22} \end{pmatrix} \begin{pmatrix} e_{1t} \\ e_{2t} \end{pmatrix} \qquad (2.3)$$

The assumption that the x vector is exogenous implies the following restrictions on the system in (2.3): $H_{11} \equiv 0$, $F_{12} \equiv 0$ and $F_{21} \equiv 0$. With these restrictions imposed, the system becomes:

$$H_{11} y_t + H_{12} x_t = F_{11} e_{1t} \qquad (2.4)$$

and:

$$H_{22} x_t = F_{22} e_{2t} \qquad (2.5)$$

From (2.4) we can solve for the so-called "transfer functions," which are different from the traditional "reduced form" equations. In the transfer functions, we have the current and lagged values of just *one* endogenous variable, and current and lagged values of the exogenous variables. In a usual reduced form equation, one current endogenous variable appears along with lagged values of it and lagged values of other endogenous variables, as well as current and lagged exogenous variables. Thus, by incorporating current and past values of just one endogenous variable, transfer functions are somewhat simpler than unrestricted reduced form equations. However, the error terms in a transfer function are usually autocorrelated even if the structural error terms are not, whereas in a traditional reduced form equation the errors are not autocorrelated, given that the structural error terms are not autocorrelated.

On multiplying each side of (2.4) by the inverse of H_{11} – namely $H_{11}^{-1} = H_{11a}/|H_{11}|$, where H_{11a} is the adjoint matrix associated with H_{11} – we obtain:

$$|H_{11}| y(t) = H_{11a} H_{12} x_t + H_{11a} F_{11} e_{lt} \qquad (2.6)$$

It is seen from (2.6) that each transfer function involves the same lag structure and parameters on the left-hand side given that there is no canceling of common roots. That is, the scalar lag polynomial, $|H_{11}|$, hits each element of $y(t)$, and thus, if there is no canceling of roots, each of the m transfer functions in (2.5) should have *identical* left-hand sides. On the right side of (2.5), if we know the orders and degrees of the matrix lag operators, the coefficients and lags on each exogenous variable in each equation can be determined algebraically. Also, the order of each moving average process on the errors in the transfer functions can be determined given information regarding the degrees of the elements of the matrix lag operators, H_{11a} and F_{11}.

Further, the marginal processes for individual variables, called the "final equations" or "marginal processes" for individual variables, can be derived by substituting $x_t = H_{22}^{-1} F_{22} e_{2t}$ from (2.5) into (2.4) to obtain $y_t = -H_{11}^{-1} H_{12} H_{22}^{-1} F_{22} e_{2t} + H_{11}^{-1} F_{11} e_{1t}$, or $|H_{11}||H_{22}| y_t = -H_{11a} H_{12} H_{22a} F_{22} e_{2t} + |H_{22}| H_{11a} F_{11} e_{1t}$. Thus, given a multivariate structural equation system in the form of (2.4) with exogenous variables generated by (2.5), it is direct to determine the forms of its associated transfer functions and final equations and check their forms using data.

As recognized and applied to a structural monetary model for the US economy, formulated and implemented by Milton Friedman, (2.6) can be employed to check formulations of dynamic structural simultaneous equations models. That is, first the equations in (2.6) are derived algebraically from the structural equations. Second, using statistical transfer identification procedures, transfer functions' forms are determined or identified empirically from the data. Then the empirically determined transfer functions' forms are compared with those of the transfer functions derived algebraically from the model. In connection with the Friedman monetary model, Palm and I found that the implied transfer functions from the model did not agree with those determined empirically from the monthly data whether we assumed adaptive expectations or rational expectations in formulating the structural equations of the model.[4] Thus there is a need for some model reformulation to have the model's transfer functions square with those determined from the data.

Similarly, we analytically derived the final equations associated with Friedman's monetary model and compared their properties with those of empirically determined univariate models for the three variables of the model: nominal money, nominal interest rate and the price level. Again, there were some discrepancies between the empirically determined final equation models and the final equations derived analytically from the structural model. While going from assumed adaptive expectations to assumed rational expectations produced some improved agreement between the empirically and analytically derived transfer functions and final equations, there is still a need for further improvement; perhaps, as we suggested, in taking better account of seasonal effects, among other elements.

Indeed, the problem of seasonality deserves much more attention in modeling daily, monthly and quarterly data. For example, when working on my doctoral dissertation years ago, I used seasonally adjusted quarterly personal disposable income and consumption data. When I wrote to Washington, DC, requesting the seasonally unadjusted quarterly personal disposable income data, I was told that "it did not exist." Baffled by this response, I wrote requesting an explanation and was told that proprietors' income was just available from income tax returns annually and was interpolated to produce quarterly estimates without incorporating a seasonal component, and thus the total income variable was not available seasonally unadjusted even though it was available seasonally adjusted. In addition to this and many other measurement problems, it is the case that seasonal adjustment procedures in use – e.g. X11, X11-ARIMA, X-12, etc. – are based on strong assumptions regarding trend, cyclical, seasonal and noise components that have little economic theoretical justification, as explained in the literature and in our report on seasonal analysis and adjustment procedures completed for the US Federal Reserve authorities.[5] In this report, in addition to statistically motivated models for seasonal analysis of monetary time series, there is an economically motivated, causal monetary model of seasonality that was formulated to provide more meaningful analyses of seasonal effects and for improved seasonal adjustment. Much more work in this area is needed and probably will yield improved analyses and predictions of the economic behavior of industries and economies. And, of course, Quenouille's multiple time series model can be generalized to incorporate seasonal effects, and associated transfer and final equations can be derived and checked for their agreement with empirically derived "seasonal" transfer functions and "seasonal" final equations.

While the above transfer functions and final equations can be derived from given, known models and compared to those derived empirically, when we do not know the form of the structural model – e.g. we do not know that the model is in the form of equation (2.4) or lack information about identifying restrictions – it is still the case that empirical work can go forward. However, here there has been a divergence of views about how to proceed. Some, including R. Litterman, C. Sims, D. Hendry and others, start with an "encompassing" or "empirical" VAR model, which is a model in the form of Quenouille's MVARMA model, perhaps with moving average (MA) error term processes of order zero – that is, the operator $F(L)$ in equation (2.1) is of degree zero. It is clearly the case that many aspects of the VAR may be unsatisfactory, and, if so, efforts to find relations that work well in forecasting will not be successful. As mentioned above, Litterman in his work showed that unrestricted VARs did not forecast very well and improved their performance by introducing informative prior densities for the parameters in his Bayesian VAR, which performed better than his unrestricted VAR but still did not provide totally acceptable performance, according to McNees' evaluation in a 1986 article in the *Journal of Business and Economic Statistics*.[6] Also, according to an article in an NIESR volume, the Bank of England carries along a BVAR model to help in its forecasting efforts, but no data are provided to evaluate its past performance.[7] And on a recent visit to the Federal Reserve Bank of Atlanta I was told that their BVAR model did not forecast very well.

When the algebraic operations above are used to derive the marginal processes for individual variables from VAR or VARMA models, the marginal processes are found to have high-order autoregressive parts and high-order MA error term processes, not very much like the low-order processes identified using Box-Jenkins and other procedures by many researchers.

Given these difficulties with complicated VAR processes and the fact that their use has not led to good point and turning point forecasts, as mentioned above, I prefer to start simply with empirically determined transfer functions or empirical univariate forecasting equations that can be derived from the data, and to evaluate their performance in forecasting experiments and in "on-line" forecasting, taking account of the preliminary data problem. If a set of equations for important variables (e.g.) the rate of growth of real GDP, the price level, the number of firms in operation, etc.) that work well in forecasting has been obtained, then it is possible to use old and new economic theory to attempt to rationalize these equations and to combine them into a logically consistent, structural econometric model capable of explaining the past and predicting the future and, possibly, being of assistance in making policy. Here the unusual fact is that certain empirical, time series relations work fairly well in explaining variation in past data and in forecasting. Explaining successfully why this is the case, using subject matter economic and statistical theory, is indeed a noteworthy and satisfying achievement and an essential element of the SEMTSA approach to model building.

As is well known, in many fields, including economics and econometrics, rationalizing empirical regularities or relationships has led to useful new models and theories. For example, Kuznets' finding of a relatively stable savings rate for the United States over the first half of the twentieth century in the face of sharply rising real income, an empirical finding contradicting Keynesian views that the savings rate would rise, led to new theories of consumer behavior by Friedman, Modigliani, Ando, Tobin and others that rationalized the constancy of the savings rate in one manner or another. However, I believe that it would be worthwhile to review Kuznets' empirical work to determine whether savings were measured appropriately. For example, as indicated in a May 23, 1987, *Wall Street Journal* article by Clark S. Judge entitled: "Problem isn't rate of US savings, but where the money goes," it was pointed out that the personal savings rate, the ratio of personal savings to personal income, "fell to an all-time low of 3.2 percent . . . in 1987." However, he pointed out that savings, as measured by the Department of Commerce, do not include much of individuals' and employers' contributions to various pension funds. Also, it was pointed out that the Department of Commerce "counts [expenditures] on cars and other consumer durable goods as consumption . . ." rather than just services yielded by durables as consumption. He pointed to a better measure of savings, the Federal Reserve's "Savings by

Individuals," which includes "all pensions and the net value of consumer durables, as well as certain capital gains that Commerce leaves out. In 1987, calculating from these figures (reported in the Council of Economic Advisers' *Economic Report to the President*), Americans saved 9.4 percent of their incomes – almost triple what Commerce shows. From 1977 to 1987 the Fed savings rate fluctuated between a low of 9 percent in 1980 to a high of 12 percent in 1984." However, that is not the end of the story, since these numbers produced by Commerce and the Federal Reserve system ". . . leave out one big contribution to savings – Social Security . . . Counting Social Security payments, we Americans sock away nearly one in every five dollars we make – 18.5 percent in 1987, up from 17.1 percent in 1980 and 17.0 percent in 1970." Also, as the author pointed out, these estimates might also have been too low because of several other items that are omitted from measured savings, namely lumping non-profit organizations, which save very little, with other individuals. "Drop out non-profits and the savings rate for individuals rises." Further, he noted that ". . . both the Fed and Commerce treat the sale of a home in a perverse way" that tends to understate the savings rate. Thus, instead of a savings rate of about 3 or 4 percent, as measured by the Department of Commerce, or a savings rate of about 9 to 12 percent, as measured by the Federal Reserve, Judge's estimate was in the range of 17 to 19 percent – much higher than Kuznets' estimates, and certainly much higher than some recently reported Department of Commerce's negative savings rates for the United States. In my opinion, this important measurement problem, undoubtedly relevant for many economies, may have a great impact on the evaluation of alternative theories of consumer savings behavior. Thus, as recognized broadly, and particularly by Richard Stone, we must be serious about measurement problems in statistics, econometrics and forecasting in order to make progress in producing statistical and econometric models that work well. Using bad data will many times produce results in accord with the old adage, "Garbage in, garbage out."

To summarize, the SEMTSA approach can be employed to check a given structural dynamic model's features by comparing its associated transfer equations and final equations properties with those determined empirically from the data using time series transfer function and final equation identification procedures. Further, the point and turning point forecasting performance of the dynamic structural model can be compared with that of empirically determined transfer and final equations. If this empirical work indicates that the structural model is defective in certain respects, then work can be undertaken to improve the original model in an iterative model improvement process, which has been employed successfully by workers in many sciences and industries.

On the other hand, if a satisfactory dynamic structural model is not available, then research is undertaken to produce relations for important, relevant variables that perform well in explaining past variation in the data and in point and turning point forecasting. Given a set of empirical relations that perform well, it is a challenge to use economic theory to explain this unusual finding. When this is done, there will usually be a number of other improvements suggested by theory that can be implemented. And of course, close study of the properties of the overall model is very worthwhile and may be done analytically and/or in simulation experiments with the model. To illustrate the importance of simulation experiments, I shall briefly review our work on a regional modeling project.

Henry Hamilton and others at the Battelle Memorial Institute (BMI) in Columbus, Ohio, along with university consultants, built a model to evaluate the possible effects of proposed dam construction by the US Corps of Engineers on the Susquehanna River on regional economic growth.[8] The Corps contracted with the National Planning Association (NPA) to estimate the effect of dam construction on the growth of the region. The NPA estimates showed a considerable impact on the growth of the region. On the other hand, the BMI model predicted very little impact over and above that associated with the direct effects of building the dams. The BMI model reflected the following very simple considerations of how dam construction might affect regional growth:

(1) Dams can provide water for irrigation in agriculture and for other heavy water-using industries;

(2) Dams can provide electric power for industrial and other uses;

(3) During low flow periods, water can be released from the dams to help deal with pollution problems that affect regional location and other decisions; and

(4) Artificial lakes created by dam construction can stimulate tourism and associated activities.

As regards these possible effects, pragmatic reasoning, and the model's outputs, reflected the fact that rainfall in the region was substantial and that agriculture in this region did not require irrigation. Also, the price of water was so low that heavy water-using industries were already in the region and would not be much affected by water's being available in connection with dam construction. As regards electricity, the region already had many sources of electricity, some hydro, at reasonable prices. With respect to pollution, the river was not very polluted and did not require released water from proposed dams to deal with pollution that, e.g., might discourage firms from locating in the region. Last, the region includes mountainous regions, the Catskills and the Poconos, with many lakes and a thriving tourist industry and didn't require artificial lakes to stimulate more tourism. These simple considerations were confirmed in the output of simulation experiments using the BMI simulation model. While the model was large to capture needed detail, its basic operation could be explained using just nine equations. Detail was added because of the use of subregions along the river, age-specific birth, migration, family formation and death rates, various industrial sectors, a water sector, etc. Having an appreciation of important, rather simple issues and considerations was extremely helpful in model building in this instance.

2.2   Application of the SEMTSA approach to macroeconomic data

The idea that structural macroeconomic models' performance in forecasting should be evaluated by comparing their performance to that of simple benchmark models is an old idea. For example, years ago during the Cowles Commission days at the University of Chicago, Milton Friedman and Carl Christ compared forecasts of Klein's models with those of random walk models, with results that were quite shocking to the structural model builders.[9] In a like manner some years later, Charles Nelson and Charles Plosser compared the forecasting performance of Box-Jenkins' ARIMA models to that of large-scale structural econometric models, with results that were again quite disturbing to the model builders.[10] The same can be said with respect to forecasts produced by Cooper's third-order autoregression, an AR(3), vis-à-vis those produced by structural econometric models.[11] The conclusions that I and many others draw from such forecasting experiments is that the structural models require reformulation to improve their forecasting performance.

Similarly, some past simulation experiments, designed to determine important properties of large-scale structural econometric models, have yielded surprising results regarding the properties of such models that were unknown to the model builders. See, for example, papers by the Adelmans and Zellner and Peck showing very unusual properties of certain large macroeconometric models.[12] Again, such results imply the need to reformulate these large, complicated models and indicate the costs of failure to KISS – that is, to keep it sophisticatedly simple.

My preference for sophisticatedly simple models should not be interpreted as just a preference for small models. If much detail is needed in modeling, a model may have to be large, but it still can be kept sophisticatedly simple. For example, as mentioned above, in modeling the Susquehanna River basin economy years ago, we needed much detail regarding subregions, different industries, etc. but managed to keep the model rather simple. This preference for simple models, and starting simply and complicating if necessary, seems to be a general one in many areas of science. As Einstein is quoted as saying, "Keep your theories as simple as possible, but no simpler." Also, Jeffreys recognized that simplicity is a relative term in discussing the Schrödinger wave equation, a partial differential equation that he regarded as "simple." What subsequent discussion brought out was that Jeffreys meant that, of the possible equations that could explain what Schrödinger wanted to explain, his equation was the simplest.

In addition to the above considerations, from the results of a St Louis Federal Reserve Bank conference in the early 1990s designed to determine which macroeconomic model (e.g. monetarist, neo-monetarist, Keynesian, neo-Keynesian, real business cycle, etc.) was best supported by the data, Ray Fair and I reported in our contributions that there was not enough empirical testing of alternative models, and explained in our papers how to proceed to formulate and test alternative macroeconomic models.[13] Of course, I emphasized the SEMTSA approach, briefly described above, as a sensible way to proceed and indicated that we had already used it to evaluate one monetary model of the United States in earlier work and were using it in current research efforts aimed at producing operational models that work well in forecasting, explanation and policy-making.

In our work to achieve this last objective, we decided to start simply and complicate if necessary. As regards the initial choice of a variable, it was decided to analyze processes for the rate of growth of real GDP, a variable of great interest to many and involved in most macroeconomic and macroeconometric models. Note that we used the first difference of the log of GDP, the growth rate, in part to get rid of systematic measurement biases and in part because there is great interest in this variable. Also, while we did some work with quarterly data in our first paper, the quality of quarterly data and seasonal adjustment procedures used in many countries leaves much to be desired, as mentioned above. In some cases quarterly data are interpolated and seasonal adjustment procedures are based on assumptions regarding trend, cyclical, seasonal and noise components – for example independence and/or stationarity assumptions – that are inappropriate for structural modeling. Thus, in the main, our empirical work has been carried forward using annual data, relating to, first, nine industrialized countries and, later, to eighteen industrialized countries. See figure 1.1 for box plots of the data.

It is seen from the box plots for the GDP growth rate data that the data reveal systematic fluctuations in the rates of growth with about a four- to six-year period – the "business cycle" observed and written about by many, with some making a distinction between "inventory" or Abramowitz cycles and longer-period "replacement" or Juglar cycles. Knowing beforehand that the data exhibited cyclical features, we decided to begin our investigations using an autoregression model of order three, which could have two imaginary roots, giving rise to a cyclical component, and a real root, giving rise to a local trend.

It didn't take very long to learn that the AR(3) model did not work well in forecasting because it was missing turning points. That is, at the top of the cycle it tended to forecast continued upward movement when the economy turned down, and at the bottom it would forecast continued contraction when the economy expanded in many cases. Note that many other time series and structural models have difficulty in forecasting turning points.

On seeing what the problem was with the AR(3) model's forecasting performance, it was not too hard to remember that Burns and Mitchell in their famous book *Measuring Business Cycles* (which I had read as a graduate student) found that money and stock prices tended to lead in the business cycle, using data for the United Kingdom, France, Germany and the United States extending back to the nineteenth century.[14] Thus, it was decided to add two variables – lagged rates of change in real money, GM, and real stock prices, SP – to our AR(3). In addition, the lagged annual rate of growth of the median of the eighteen countries' rates of growth of real stock prices was introduced as a world return variable, WSP, to obtain the following equation for the i'th country:

$$y_{it} = \beta_{0i} + \beta_{1i} y_{it-1} + \beta_{2i} y_{it-2} + \beta_{3i} y_{it-3} + \beta_{4i} GM_{it-1}$$
$$+ \beta_{5i} SP_{it-1} + \beta_{6i} SP_{it-2} + \beta_{7i} WSP_{t-1} + u_{it}$$
$$i = 1, 2, \ldots, m \quad t = 1, 2, \ldots, T \quad (2.7a)$$

or:

$$y_i = X_i \beta_i + u_i \quad (2.7b)$$

As explained in my first lecture, we rationalized the introduction of the lagged rate of change of real money by pointing to the real balance effects of the classical quantity theory of money. That is, changes in real money tend to induce increased expenditures in order for producers and consumers to achieve a new equilibrium in their portfolios of various financial and real assets. In earlier studies using US data, I estimated such real balance effects in quarterly consumption functions and found significant effects, which were reproduced using British data.[15] Also, on disaggregation, in an unpublished paper, it was found for consumers that changes in real money holdings tended to affect real expenditures on durable goods and services much more than real expenditures on non-durables.[16]

The introduction of the leading indicator stock return variable was rationalized by pointing out that the stock market reacts quickly to news events (e.g. wars, policy changes, unexpected changes in oil prices, etc.) whereas the economy reacts with a lag, perhaps due to delays and costs associated with changing the values of real variables. In general, the introduction of the "leading indicator" variables in our model, now called an autoregressive, leading indicator model, led to better fits, but not over-fits, and more accurate forecasts.

At this stage in our work, we distributed our data set to those who requested it. One group used our data set and found that their estimation and forecasting techniques, based on various state space models, worked "much, much better" in terms of the RMSEs of forecast than our model. Their RMSEs were so low that I knew that something had to be wrong. Finally, it occurred to me that perhaps they had used the complete sample to fit their model and used part of the same sample in their forecasting experiments. It turned out that this was indeed what they had done, and when this "glitch" was corrected their RMSEs increased substantially and did not dominate those of the ARLI model. Another researcher, S. Mittnik, used our data in conjunction with his clever model identification procedures and found that we should have included not only the real money growth rate with a one-year lag but also the same variable with a two-year lag.[17] Also, he found that no lagged values of the output growth rate were needed in his empirically determined relation. Further, his state space methods produced forecasts that seemed rather good. Last, P. W. Otter used our data and canonical correlation methods to obtain yet another preferred model, namely one in which output growth was linked to the output growth rate and the growth rates of real money, real stock returns and world stock returns, all lagged one year.[18]

In view of these different results about what the appropriate model is, I thought it of interest to consider all possible models, involving the eight input variables, that is, $2^8 = 256$ possible models, including our formulation as well as those of Mittnik and Otter. That is, posterior odds were computed relating to particular models versus the broadest model, that containing all eight input variables using the expression for posterior odds that a former student, A. Siow, and I had derived and applied earlier. The posterior odds favored our AR(3)LI model, the Mittnik and Otter models, and a few others. Indeed, the results indicated that our AR(3)LI model was slightly favored relative to the Mittnik and Otter models, and all three models were strongly favored relative to a random walk model and somewhat favored relative to the general model containing all eight input variables.[19]

A surprise that came out of these calculations was the high posterior odds favoring several models that just included the rate of output lagged three years while excluding values of this variable lagged one and two years. The odds favored these restricted AR(3)LI models quite markedly even though their advantage in terms of RMSEs of forecast was not that great. It turns out on further analysis that an autoregression $y(t) = a + by(t - 3)$, with $b < 0$, can have one real root and two complex roots with an associated cycle of about five to six years; just about right for our problem. Thus, the added complexity of including the variables $y(t - 1)$ and $y(t - 2)$ does not appear to be necessary to produce an appropriate cyclical component.

These posterior odds calculations gave us information that our specification of the ARLI model was competitive relative to the alternatives suggested by Mittnik and Otter, as well as to many other formulations in the 255 alternatives to our model. However, the RMSEs of forecast for all the models seemed too large, even though they were much smaller than those for random walk and other benchmark models, and thus there was a need for further improvement. As noted by many, posterior odds constitute a relative measure, not an absolute measure, of performance. For example, the posterior odds on model A versus model B might be thirty to one, but this does not imply that A is an adequate model. It may be that B is a very bad model and that A is just a poor model. It was for these reasons that we computed RMSEs of forecast to get some idea of the absolute performance of our models.

To achieve model improvement, we considered a variety of possible alternatives, including (1) adding the current rate of growth of a 'world' real income variable – the annual median output growth rate of the eighteen countries in our sample – to our ARLI model, renamed the ARLI/WI model, and (2) adding an equation to explain and forecast the median growth rates of the eighteen countries, which are plotted in figure 1.1 Note that the median of the eighteen countries' growth rates follows a cyclical path and, of course, a real world income variable is an important element in the demand for countries' exports.

Using the ARLI/WI model, we first forecasted the median growth rate of the eighteen countries and then inserted this forecasted growth rate in the eighteen countries' individual ARLI/WI equations and used them to forecast countries' output growth rates year by year. Generally, the ARLI/WI model performed better than the individual countries' ARLI models without the world income variable. Later, R. A. Highfield and J. Tobias indicated that a joint analysis of the equations for individual countries involving the world income variable and the equation for world income was possible, and their results certainly deserve more attention in future work.[20]

In addition to experimenting with the ARLI and ARLI/WI models, we also investigated several alternative "pooling" or "shrinkage" procedures, building on the work of Stein and our earlier work on Bayesian statistical shrinkage techniques. Briefly, in the 1920s actuarial statisticians had discovered empirically that, when estimating many parameters relating to different insured groups, it was useful to average individuals' estimates with an estimate of an overall mean. Essentially, the individual estimates were being drawn closer or "shrunk" towards the common estimated mean, and results seemed more "stable" and "useful" than estimates obtained without averaging or shrinking.

In the 1950s, Charles Stein, an eminent statistician, published theoretical work based on the Bayesian approach that theoretically implied a posterior mean in a form similar to the "shrinkage" estimates used by the actuarial statisticians. He further showed that not only does the shrinkage procedure effect improvement relative to other, traditional procedures under special conditions, but that, when quadratic loss is used, shrinkage procedures uniformly dominate usual estimation procedures, including least squares and maximum likelihood procedures, when estimating a vector of three or more means or a vector of three or more regression coefficients, etc. Thus, the usual, maximum likelihood and least squares estimators are inadmissible relative to Stein's shrinkage estimators – a finding that shook the profession.

The added information that individual means are distributed about a common mean, or that elements of a regression model's coefficients are distributed about a common value, is extremely useful in improving performance of both estimators and predictors for a wide range of models and is often compatible with empirical conditions. In view of these developments and my own work joint with a former student, Walter Vandaele, on interpreting and producing Stein-like estimators for various problems using Bayesian and non-Bayesian procedures,[21] it was decided to investigate the extent to which Stein-like shrinking or pooling would help improve the forecasting performance of our ARLI and ARLI/WI models.

A second modification of our original fixed parameter ARLI model was to make allowance for parameter variation through time, much in the way that engineers do in their state space models; see, e.g., the useful books by Swamy, and Kim and Nelson, for consideration and analysis of a variety of time-varying parameter models.[22] Now, it may be asked, "Why should parameters of macroeconomic models vary through time?" There are many reasons, namely aggregation effects, structural changes or breaks, technological change, changes in tastes, changes in economic policies and their attendant effects on parameters – so-called "Lucas effects," etc. It is indeed surprising that not very many models in the macroeconometric area involve the use of time-varying parameters. Indeed, in a recent review of a leading book on economic forecasting, published in 1999, the well-known forecaster L.-E. Öller remarked, "State space models would have fitted in here [in modeling breaks], but are not considered."

A question that naturally arises in attempting to model time-varying parameters is, "How do the parameters vary?" One point of view that we considered briefly was to assume that parameters might change at specific points in the business cycle and that a Markov process might be used to model such specific changes. Since such an approach would involve introducing many parameters and might not capture the properties of the timing of parameter changes and the nature of their movements, we decided to follow the state space engineers' approach by making the parameters random and putting specific time series processes on them that permit them to vary using relatively few parameters. Thus, for example, in our first published paper in 1987, we assumed that the coefficient vector in the ARLI model for the i'th country β_{it} followed a vector random walk $\beta_{it} = \beta_{it-1} + \varepsilon_{it}$, $t = 1, 2, \ldots, T$, $i = 1, 2, \ldots, m$.

Using recursive computing procedures, we were able to utilize this random walk process along with the data to produce one-year-ahead forecasts. Also, broader processes for the parameter vectors were employed, along with shrinkage assumptions. For example, in one model we assumed that the i'th country's coefficient vector was distributed around a common vector θ_t that is allowed to follow a vector random walk. That is, we assumed $\beta_{it} = \theta_t + \varepsilon_{it}$, where θ_t is a common mean in year t, ε_{it} an error vector and $\theta_t = \theta_{t-1} + u_t$ a vector random walk for the annual common mean parameter vector θ_t. Recursive Bayesian updating procedures were used to estimate and forecast year by year. Such models were termed time-varying parameter, ARLI models, and denoted by TVP/ARLI. When similar assumptions and techniques were applied to our ARLI/WI models, we called the resulting models TVP/ARLI/WI models. In the case of such models, we fitted them country by country with no shrinkage or pooling assumptions and with such assumptions.

In table 2.1 forecasting results using fixed parameters and time-varying parameters with and without pooling are shown. In the upper panel, forecasting results for the eighteen countries using TVP/ARLI/WI models with and without pooling are presented. It is seen that, when pooling is utilized, countries' RMSEs of forecast are more highly concentrated about a lower median value, namely 1.74 percentage points, than when pooling is not utilized, namely 2.37 percentage points.

Similar results are encountered when shrinkage is employed using FP models, namely a median RMSE = 1.86 percentage points when the pooling or shrinkage assumption is employed, as against a median RMSE = 2.60 percentage points when the pooling or shrinkage assumption is not employed. Also, results for the TVP models are slightly

Table 2.1 *Forecasted RMSEs and MAEs for disaggregated models using currency as money variable (percentage points), 1952–79 ⇒ 1980–97*

Error	AR(3)(DA)	AR(3)LI(DA)	Distrib Lag(DA)	MMM(DA) I	II	III	IV
			OLS				
RMSE	2.26	1.62	1.61	1.61	1.52	1.47	1.80
MAE	1.65	1.32	1.35	1.31	1.28	1.25	1.47
			Extended MELO				
RMSE	2.26	1.58	1.62	1.55	1.55	1.50	1.80
MAE	1.65	1.23	1.34	1.26	1.31	1.26	1.46
			2SLS				
RMSE	2.26	1.60	1.63	1.59	1.49	1.48	1.78
MAE	1.65	1.31	1.38	1.29	1.25	1.24	1.45
			SUR				
RMSE	2.21	1.70	1.66	1.68	1.61	1.40	1.92
MAE	1.52	1.41	1.36	1.39	1.38	1.17	1.60
			Complete shrinkage				
RMSE	2.11	1.73	1.82	1.76	1.57	1.59	1.70
MAE	1.45	1.57	1.60	1.46	1.37	1.38	1.43
		γ-shrinkage ($\gamma = 0$, same as OLS above): $\gamma = 0.25$					
RMSE	2.21	1.62	1.61	1.61	1.49	1.46	1.74
MAE	1.59	1.36	1.38	1.34	1.26	1.25	1.41
			$\gamma = 0.5$				
RMSE	2.18	1.62	1.63	1.62	1.49	1.46	1.71
MAE	1.56	1.39	1.42	1.36	1.27	1.27	1.38
			$\gamma = 1$				
RMSE	2.15	1.64	1.66	1.64	1.49	1.48	1.69
MAE	1.52	1.44	1.46	1.38	1.29	1.29	1.39
			$\gamma = 2$				
RMSE	2.13	1.66	1.70	1.67	1.51	1.50	1.68
MAE	1.49	1.48	1.51	1.41	1.32	1.32	1.40
			$\gamma = 5$				
RMSE	2.11	1.69	1.75	1.71	1.53	1.54	1.68
MAE	1.47	1.52	1.56	1.44	1.34	1.35	1.41

better than those for the FP models. Thus, improvements in forecasting performance were encountered using the TVP/ARLI/WI model with pooling assumptions.

To effect further improvements in forecasting performance, the possibility of using "combined forecasts" from several alternative models was considered. Or one may refer to this as a form of model averaging. For many years in the forecasting literature since the publication of the innovative paper by Bates and Granger, there has been much research on how to combine different forecasts and whether the combining of forecasts tends to improve forecasts.[23] See R. Clemens' paper for a comprehensive review of research on these and other topics relating to forecast combining techniques and their uses.[24] First, there is the issue of whether combining or averaging alternative forecasts will always produce improved forecasts. Since "always" is a very strong word, I was skeptical that combining would always improve forecasts. Simply, if we average a bad forecast with a very good one, it is not at all clear that we always get improved forecasting performance by using the average. In work with Palm and Min, it was shown that, when the forecasts being considered do not constitute an exhaustive set and they may be biased, it is not the case that combining forecasts always produces improved results.[25] Sometimes it does, but not always.

Further, there is the issue of how to combine alternative forecasts. Some ingenious Bayesian and non-Bayesian procedures in the literature due to Winkler, Granger, Bates and others are based on the assumption that the forecasts to be combined are all unbiased – a very strong assumption. There are many reasons that may cause forecasts to be biased, e.g. use of defective models, bad data, asymmetric predictive loss functions for which biased forecasts are optimal, etc.

In view of this restriction of unbiasedness on forecasts to be combined and other reasons mentioned above, we did not believe with certainty that combining forecasts derived from different models would always lead to improvement. However, since there is a possibility that improvement might result and since we wished to compare Bayesian and non-Bayesian combining techniques, it was thought worthwhile to investigate the issues of whether it pays to combine and how to combine most effectively.

In the Bayesian approach to combining, first we compute the posterior odds on alternative models – say, an FP model versus a TVP model. Then, as I suggested in a 1987 paper, it is possible to derive a "combining density" that is closest in a weighted information metric sense to the individual predictive densities of alternative models.[26] That is, if two predictive densities for a future observation y_f are available – say, $f_1(y_f)$ and $f_2(y_f)$ – with associated posterior probabilities P_1 and P_2, the weighted Euclidean distance between these densities and a combining density, $y_c(y_f)$, can be minimized by choice of f_c subject to f_c's being proper to yield the optimal result, f_c^*: namely $f_c^* = a[K f_1 + f_2]$, where a = normalizing constant and $K = P_1/P_2$. Of course, other distance metrics can be employed in deriving optimal combining densities. Also, more than two densities can be combined using a given distance metric.

Given a combining density, for example that shown above, it can be employed to make probability statements about future outcomes, e.g. to compute the probability that next year's growth rate will be below this year's growth rate, etc. Also, given whatever predictive loss function is thought to be appropriate, point predictions that minimize expected predictive loss can be determined, analytically or numerically, and employed in forecasting.

Posterior odds can be utilized to compare a combining density and a given predictive density – say, that associated with a benchmark model or a particular model – in a model choice context. Thus, in some years a benchmark model and its forecast may be employed, and in others the combined density and its forecast are employed. This procedure was applied in forecasting eighteen industrialized countries' output growth rates, and it was found that use of this model choice approach did not yield much improvement relative to general use of the combined forecasts or general use of the forecasts of any particular model.[27] Thus, while combining and model choice approaches can provide improved results, it is not the case that they always do so.

Obtaining the posterior odds on FP versus TVP models took some hard work, but finally the result was obtained in an easily computable manner that could be used to derive the optimal combining density, the mean of which was an optimal point forecast relative to quadratic loss.

In evaluating the actual performance of such combined forecasts vis-à-vis individual forecasts, it was found in our examples that combining did not produce much in the way of improved forecasts but that our Bayesian combining procedures worked better than the non-Bayesian combining techniques we considered.

As a result of the above investigations, it was concluded that the TVP/ARLI/WI model utilizing pooling or shrinkage techniques was the model that worked best in point forecasting of annual rates of growth of real output for eighteen industrial countries. Then the issue arose as to how well this model, and variants of it, would work in forecasting turning points in countries' real growth rates; that is, in forecasting downturns and upturns in output growth rates for these countries. As explained in the first lecture, we (1) defined turning points, (2) derived probabilities of a downturn and of no downturn, P_{DT} and $P_{NDT} = 1 - P_{DT}$ respectively, from models' predictive densities, and (3) used these probabilities along with a 2×2 loss structure to derive optimal turning point forecasts. That is, given two possible outcomes – say, DT or NDT – we chose the forecast – say, a DT – that has lower, associated expected loss. On applying this approach using a symmetric loss structure, the optimal procedure is to forecast a DT if the probability of a DT is greater than $\frac{1}{2}$. If the probability of a DT is less than $\frac{1}{2}$, the optimal forecast is NDT. Similar analysis, along with a definition of an upturn and no upturn for outcomes at the bottom of a cyclical episode, leads to an optimal choice between UT and NUT forecasts that can easily be computed. Again, if the 2×2 loss structure is symmetric, it is optimal to forecast an UT when the probability of an upturn is greater than $\frac{1}{2}$ and NUT when it is less than $\frac{1}{2}$. On applying these techniques to the data for eighteen industrialized countries using a variety of models, with and without pooling, results were obtained that indicate that our various models forecasted 70 percent or more of 211 turning point episodes correctly! What a pleasant surprise. In connection with almost all models considered, use of pooling or shrinkage tended to produce improved results.

Also, results of experiments with asymmetric loss functions show that, by altering the relative costs of errors, it is possible to improve certain forecasts.[28] That is, when the cost of an erroneous NDT forecast is high, such forecasts are made just when the evidence for an NDT outcome is extremely strong and thus the percentage of correct NDT forecasts tends to rise. This is important to recognize since in many circumstances an incorrect NDT forecast can be a much more serious error than an incorrect DT forecast. Thus, choice of an appropriate loss structure is very important. Further, it should be recognized that it is possible to choose among more complicated alternatives, e.g. a moderate downturn, a severe downturn and no downturn, and similarly with respect to upturns. Using various 3×3 loss structures, optimal turning point forecasts were computed and reported in a recent paper.[29] It was found that it is difficult, but not impossible, to forecast the more detailed outcomes.

Some of our work on forecasting turning points was made known to Milton Friedman. He challenged us to expand the forecasting time period to increase the number of turning point episodes. We took up his challenge by expanding our sample to increase the number of turning point episodes from 158 to 211.[30] Fortunately, the models continued to forecast about 70 percent or more of the turning points successfully, and much better than a variety of naïve turning point forecasters, e.g. a coin flipper, or an "eternal optimist," who always forecasts NDT at the top and UT at the bottom, or an "eternal pessimist," who always forecasts DT at the top and NUT at the bottom.

Above, we have used likelihood functions based on the assumption that error terms and data are normally distributed. In recent works, we have used the Bayesian method of moments, which does not involve the use of a likelihood function or prior density in obtaining post data densities for parameters and predictive densities for future observations. As explained above, various assumptions are made about the moments of the realized error or disturbance terms in relations that imply values of the moments of parameters. Then, on making assumptions about the moments of future, as yet unobserved error terms, given the moments of the parameters, the moments of future values of the dependent variable – say, the rate of growth – can be derived and used in forecasting. Also, given the moments, proper maxent densities are easily obtained, which are useful in making probability statements about future growth rates and deriving turning point forecasts. In this work, as mentioned earlier, Tobias, Ryu and I extended the possible outcomes to include moderate DT, extreme DT and NDT, and we were able to determine an optimal forecast using a 3×3 loss function and computed probabilities associated with the possible outcomes. Also, results of experiments with the use of bounds on future growth rates, e.g. Hicks-like ceilings and floors, were reported. Overall, the results indicated that the BMOM approach is operational and yields rather good results with minimal assumptions.

See my paper with Tobias for detailed comparisons of BMOM and traditional Bayesian (TB) results relating to the multiple regression model.[31] In this paper, posterior odds are calculated that can be used to compare and/or combine TB and BMOM posterior and predictive densities. As mentioned in the first lecture, the BMOM is an example of a new, operational Bayesian information processing, inference procedure that can be employed when the likelihood function's and/or the prior density's forms are not known.

2.3   Models and economic theory

Now, with the statistical models mentioned above that worked fairly well in fitting past data and in point and turning point forecasting, the next step in our continuing efforts to improve our models was to check the compatibility of our models with macroeconomic theory. In this connection, we showed that it is possible to derive our ARLI/WI model from a standard aggregate demand and supply model. Also, Chansik Hong in his doctoral dissertation showed that it is possible to derive the ARLI/WI model from a variant of a Hicksian IS/LM model, for many years the standard model featured in many macroeconomic texts.[32] Later, Chung-ki Min in his doctoral dissertation showed that our ARLI/WI model can be derived from a generalized real business cycle model that he formulated.[33] These derivations are examples of "going from the data to the theory," which is very often the case in science.

While the aforementioned compatibility with various economic theoretical models was satisfying, it was recognized that these models were not adequate to describe many empirical features of business fluctuations and growth as described in Burns and Mitchell's work and in various business cycle textbooks. Thus, a need to go beyond these theoretical models was recognized. Below, there is a discussion of disaggregation and modeling of economies, followed by a description of the Marshallian macroeconomic model and its statistical and econometric implementation and performance in some forecasting experiments.

Disaggregation and the Marshallian macroeconomic model

The idea that disaggregation may help to improve the explanatory and predictive performance of models is an old one, emphasized particularly in the work of Richard Stone, Guy Orcutt and others. Remarkably, there is not an extensive analytical and empirical literature on the possible improvements in forecasting provided by disaggregation. In a working paper co-authored with Enrique de Alba, we analyzed the aggregation of regression models under various conditions to show when there would be gains in forecasting precision by forecasting components of an aggregate variable and adding the forecasts of components to get a forecast of the total.[34] Generally, it is when the input variables to the individual regression equations are highly negatively correlated that the greatest gains are realized using disaggregation. If the input variables for individual equations are identical, there is no gain associated with disaggregation. See also the impressive analytical results of Lütkepohl for the effects of disaggregation in the context of forecasting stationary time series. Further, in Antonio Espasa's empirical forecasting of inflation rates, he reports that forecasting the components of inflation – that is, rates of change of prices for various sectors – and summing them to get an overall inflation rate forecast has provided much improved forecasts relative to those based on analyses of aggregate price level data.[35] Thus, there is some analytical and empirical evidence that not only can disaggregation provide valuable information about and forecasts for sectors of economies but it may also lead to better forecasts of aggregate variables.

As described in the first lecture, the idea of disaggregating by sector with a Marshallian model for each sector occurred to me a few years ago. The idea appealed to me very much since the Marshallian industry model, with its demand, supply *and* entry relations, has been one of the most successful economic models. Also, William Veloce, a former doctoral student of mine, and I had used it in analyzing data for the Canadian furniture industry, with rather interesting results. In particular, the annual changes in the number of firms in operation was much greater than we expected and had a substantial impact on industry supply, which is often overlooked in models that just include demand and supply equations with no allowance for the number of firms in operation and entry and exit effects. Indeed, the failure to include the number of firms in operation in supply equations and to take account of firm failures and start-ups is a serious defect of many econometric models of industries and economies, and mathematical economists' general equilibrium models. As I have emphasized in past writing, some supposed partial adjustment supply equations giving rise to lagged responses may be confusing lags in entry behavior with lags in supply response, as pointed out in one of my general articles on the SEMTSA approach.[36] Recognition that shutdown and start-up decisions are very important components of the process of moving from one equilibrium to another led to the inclusion of an entry equation in our Marshallian sector model. The other two equations are simply formulated consumer demand and industry supply equations.

In formulating our model of a sector, in line with my belief in starting simply and complicating if necessary, the first model – a slightly modified version of that considered in my earlier work with Veloce – is a simple one that can be generalized in many directions, if necessary.[37] Starting with a competitive industry in which each producer uses a Cobb-Douglas production function $q = AL^\alpha K^\beta$, where q = output, L = labor input, K = capital service input and $A = A_1 A_2^\alpha A_3^\beta$, the product of neutral and factor-augmenting technical change effects, and $0 < \alpha + \beta < 1$. Then the profit function is $\pi = pq - wL - rK$, where p, w and r are the real prices of output, labor and capital services that are given to the competitive firm. On maximizing profits with respect to L and K to obtain the profit-maximizing inputs L^* and K^*, the firm's supply function is $q = AL^{*\alpha} L^{*\beta}$. On multiplying both sides by the number of firms in operation at time t, N, and the real price of output, p, the industry "real sales" supply equation is $S = Npq = NA^* p^{1/\theta} w^{-\alpha/\theta} \gamma^{-\beta/\theta}$. On logging both sides and differentiating with respect to time, the industry real sales supply relation is:

$$\dot{S}/S = \dot{N}/N + \dot{A}^*/A^* + (1/\theta)\dot{p}/p - (\alpha/\theta)\dot{w}/w$$
$$- (\beta/\theta)\dot{r}/r \quad \text{SUPPLY} \tag{2.8}$$

where $A^* = A^{1/\theta}$ and dots over variables denote time derivatives, e.g. $\dot{N} = dN / dt$.

Similarly, we express the consumer demand equation in terms of real sales; that is, $S = pq = Bp^{1-\eta} x_1^{\eta_1} x_2^{\eta_2} \cdots x_k^{\eta_k}$, where the parameters B and η are non-negative and the x's are "demand shifters" such as real disposable income, real money balances, etc. On logging this "real sales" demand equation and differentiating with respect to time, the result is:

$$\dot{S}/S = (1 - \eta)\dot{p}/p + \sum_{i=1}^{k} \eta_i \dot{x}_i/x_i \quad \text{DEMAND} \qquad (2.9)$$

Finally, our entry equation is $\dot{N}/N = \gamma'(\Pi - F_e)$, where γ' is a positive adjustment parameter, Π is industry profits and F_e is a fixed real cost of entry. Since $\Pi = \theta S$ from our Cobb-Douglas model, the entry relation can be written as:

$$\dot{N}/N = \gamma'(\Pi - F_e) = \gamma(S - F) \quad \text{ENTRY} \qquad (2.10)$$

where $\gamma = \gamma'\theta$ and $F = F_e/\theta$.

There are three endogenous variables in the above model, namely S, p and N. In line with our SEMTSA approach for discrete time systems, we solve the above continuous model for the transfer function for the rate of change of real sales, $(1/S)dS/dt$, by substituting from equation (2.10) in (2.8) and then eliminating $\dot{p}/p$ from the two equations, to obtain:

$$\dot{S}/S = a(1 - S/F) + g \qquad (2.11)$$

where g is a linear combination of the rates of growth of demand- and supply-shifting variables, e.g. real income, real balances, real wage rate, real price of capital services, etc.

The form of the continuous transfer equation for S in (2.11) is surprising in that, for constant g, it is in the form of the differential equation the solution of which is the well-known logistic function, which has been fitted by many to output data for many industries and also employed in the marketing literature in connection with modeling sales of new products. Note that for $g = 0$, from the phase diagram considerations, $S = F = S_e$ is an equilibrium. If $S > S_e$, $dS/dt < 0$, while if $S < S_e$, $dS/dt > 0$, and thus the equilibrium is stable. For temporary variations in g, S will return to S_e. Further, if S on the right-hand side of equation (2.11) has a discrete lag, i.e. $S = S(t - 1)$, then the return to equilibrium can involve oscillations. Further, a discrete approximation to (2.11) is well known to be in the form of a chaotic model.[38] Thus (2.11) is indeed a rather appealing and useful initial formulation.

Now, if a sector model such as that described above is available for each sector of an economy, it is possible to aggregate labor, capital and other input factor demands over the sectors to get economy-wide factor demands for labor, capital and other inputs that, when combined with labor, capital and other input supply equations, can determine factor prices, factor utilization and factor payments. In an open economy, a foreign sector would have to be added along with a government sector to complete the MMM.

It is, of course, recognized that many variants of the above sector model are possible. For example, monopolistic competition might be assumed rather than perfect competition. Interdependencies between or among sectors through demand or supply of materials can be introduced. However, before considering all these possible complications, it was thought interesting to check the extent to which the simple model above was useful in forecasting.

Model specification, estimation and forecasting

To make the above sector model operational, a discrete approximation to the continuous transfer equation in (2.11) was formulated,[39] namely:

$$y_{1t} = y_{2t}\gamma_2 + y_{3t}\gamma_3 + x'_{1t}\beta_1 + u_{1t} \qquad (2.12)$$

where $y_{1t} = (1 - L)\log S_t$, $y_{2t} = (1 - L)\log W_t$, $y_{3t} = (1 - L)\log Y_t$, with S_t real sector sales, W_t real wage rate and Y_t real GDP, and

$x'_{1t} = (1, S_{t-1}, S_{t-2}, S_{t-3}, (1 - L) \log SR_{t-1}, (1 - L)M_{t-1})$ with SR_t real stock prices and M_t real money. In equation (2.12) it is possible that y_{2t} and y_{3t} are exogenous variables. With equations like (2.12) for each sector, with the real wage rate and real GDP variables assumed exogenous, we have a set of dynamic seemingly unrelated regression equations, since we would expect error terms to be contemporaneously correlated across sectors. However, it should be realized that the assumptions regarding the income and wage rate variables as being exogenous to the sector may not be satisfied. Thus, below, we also consider models in which they are considered to be endogenous variables. We have not as yet computed posterior odds on the hypothesis of exogeneity versus endogeneity – a procedure that would permit us to use one or the other of the hypotheses or average over the alternative models.

On the other hand, if y_2 and y_3 in equation (2.12) are endogenous variables, simultaneous equations complications are present. In this case, the following MMM reduced form equations for the three endogenous variables in (2.12) are:

$$y_1 = X\pi_1 + v_1 \qquad (2.13)$$

and:

$$Y_1 = X\Pi_1 + V_1 \qquad (2.14)$$

where $Y_1 = (y_2, y_3)$ and $X = (X_1, X_0)$, where X_0 contains predetermined variables in the system that are not included in equation (2.12).

Clearly, with a simultaneous equations model for each sector in the form of (2.12), the system can be jointly estimated and used for forecasting – a procedure that has not as yet been implemented. What has been done in the case that simultaneous equation complications are present is to substitute from (2.14) in (2.12) to obtain the well-known restricted reduced form equation:

$$y_1 = X\Pi_1\gamma_1 + X_1\beta_1 + v_1 = \bar{Z}\delta_1 + v_1 \qquad (2.15)$$

with $\bar{Z} = (X\Pi_1 \vdots X_1)$ and $\delta_1' = (\gamma_1' \vdots \beta_1')$, and where v_1 is a reduced form error vector.

To estimate the coefficients in (2.15), in the Bayesian literature, "goodness of fit", "precision of estimation" and "balanced loss" functions have been employed.[40] In each case, optimal structural coefficient estimates that are associated with minimum expected loss are available for use, and they have been found to have rather good sampling properties in Monte Carlo experiments.[41]

In table 2.2 the three loss functions mentioned in the previous paragraph are presented, along with the optimal Bayesian estimates using a TB approach and a BMOM approach. In the TB approach, a normal likelihood function for the reduced form system in equation (2.14) and a diffuse prior for its parameters are employed to obtain a posterior density for the reduced form parameters that is employed to evaluate the expectations of the three loss functions. In the BMOM approach, there is no use of an assumed likelihood function or prior density, but rather assumptions are introduced regarding the properties of the realized error terms that imply values of the parameters' moments, which can be used to evaluate the optimal, minimal expected loss (MELO) estimates that are shown in table 2.2. Surprisingly, these optimal Bayesian estimates turn out to be in the form of "K" or "double K" class estimates put forward years ago in the econometric literature. For years, work was directed at the problem of how to choose values for the K parameters. Fortunately, the Bayesian approach automatically provides optimal values when diffuse prior information is employed. Of course, if more informative prior densities for parameters are employed, the optimal estimates will no longer be in the form of K or double K class estimates.

Table 2.2 *Bayesian minimum expected loss structural coefficient estimates[a]*

Loss function	BMOM approach	Diffuse prior, normal likelihood function, traditional Bayesian approach[b]
1. Goodness of fit: $L_g = (y_1 - \bar{Z}_1\delta_1)'(y_1 - \bar{Z}_1\hat{\delta}_1)$	$K_1 = 1 - k/(n-k)$ $K_2 = 1$	$K_1 = 1 - k/(n-k-m_1-2)$ $K_2 = 1$
2. Precision of estimation: $L_p = (\hat{\delta}_1 - \delta_1)'\bar{Z}_1\bar{Z}_1(\hat{\delta}_1 - \delta_1)$	$K_1 = K_2 = 1 - k/(n-k)$	$K_1 = K_2 = 1 - k/(n-k-m_1-2)$
3. Balanced or extended loss function: $L_b = \omega L_g + (1-\omega)L_p$	$K_1 = 1 - k/(n-k)$ $K_2 = 1 - (1-\omega)k/(n-k)$	$K_1 = 1 - k/(n-k-m_1-2)$ $K_2 = 1 - (1-\omega)k/(n-k-m_1-2)$

[a] The MELO estimates are in the form of K class or double K class estimates, i.e.

$$\hat{\delta}_1(K_1, K_2) = \begin{bmatrix} Y_1'Y_1 - K_1\hat{V}_1'\hat{V}_1 & Y_1'X_1 \\ X_1'Y_1 & X_1'X_1 \end{bmatrix}^{-1} \begin{bmatrix} (Y_1 - K_2\hat{V}_1)'y_1 \\ X_1'y_1 \end{bmatrix}$$

The parameters $\delta_1' = (\gamma_1', \beta_1')$ in the following structural equation are estimated by $\hat{\delta}_1(K_1, K_2)$:

$$\underset{n \times 1}{y_1} = \underset{n \times m_1}{Y_1} \underset{m_1 \times 1}{\gamma_1} + \underset{n \times k_1}{X_1} \underset{k_1 \times 1}{\beta_1} + \underset{n \times 1}{u_1^*}$$

with $Y_1 = X\Pi_1 + V_1$, the reduced form equations for Y_1, $\hat{V}_1 = Y_1 - X\hat{\Pi}_1$ and $\hat{\Pi}_{11} = (X'X)^{-1}X'Y_1$.

[b] See Zellner (1978, 1997a) for derivation of these results.

Further, note that the elements of v_1 in equation (2.13) may be correlated with the elements of V_1 in (2.14). If we consider the regression of v_1 on V_1, $v_1 = V_1\eta_1 + \varepsilon_1$, and substitute this expression for v_1 in (2.15), we have:

$$y_1 = X\Pi_1\gamma_1 + X_1\beta_1 + (Y_1 - X\Pi_1)\eta_1 + \varepsilon_1 \qquad (2.16a)$$

or:

$$y_1 = \overline{W}_1\delta_1 + \varepsilon_1 \qquad (2.16b)$$

where $\overline{W}_1 = (X\Pi_1, X_1, Y_1 - X\Pi_1)$ and $\delta_1' = (\gamma_1', \beta_1', \eta_1)$. To estimate the coefficient vector δ_1, we can use the "goodness of fit," "precision of estimation" or "balanced loss" functions shown in table 2.2 and compute optimal estimates. Also, as explained in my paper with B. Chen, a complete posterior density for the parameters in (2.16b) and a predictive density and optimal forecasts for future values of y_1 can be computed.[42]

Another variant of the problem is one in which we have a set of restricted reduced form equations, say for the demand, supply and entry sector equations, each in the form of (2.16). It is possible to compute joint posterior densities for the system's parameters and predictive densities that take account of the error term correlations. Also, optimal point estimates and predictions vis-à-vis given loss functions can be computed.

All of the above finite sample Bayesian results contrast markedly with the available non-Bayesian estimation techniques for simultaneous equations systems. For example, there is no known optimal finite sample estimator for parameters of a structural equation. All estimators are generally rationalized in terms of asymptotic criteria, e.g. consistency, asymptotic unbiasedness, asymptotic efficiency, etc. – properties also enjoyed by Bayesian estimators. In terms of the two-stage least squares (2SLS) estimate, note that, for the "goodness of fit" loss function, if one were to conditionalize by inserting $\Pi_1 = \hat{\Pi}_1$ – the least squares estimate of Π_1 – the minimizing value is the 2SLS estimate. However, this estimate is just a conditional minimizing estimate, not an unconditional minimizing estimate. Similarly, in Basmann's generalized classical linear estimator, there is a conditioning on an estimate of the reduced form coefficients, and the resulting estimator is rationalized in terms or asymptotic properties, not exact finite sample properties.

Note that, in equation (2.16b), conditional upon Π_1, it is in the form of a regression model and this feature can be exploited in obtaining finite sample posterior densities for its parameters and predictive densities for future observations, These results can be employed to analyze (2.16b) alone or as one of a set of relations with correlated errors; that is, in the form of a non-linear SUR system.

That the Bayesian approach yields exact finite sample results for the individual equations and the joint non-linear SUR system is remarkable. And, of course, the usual large sample properties of posterior densities – namely that they are normally shaped with mean equal to the maximum likelihood estimate and variance-covariance matrix equal to the inverse of the estimated Fisher information matrix – hold in the above case, and thus in large samples there will be agreement with likelihood results, as proved by Jeffreys, Heyde and Johnstone, Chen and others.[43] However, in small to moderate-sized samples, optimal Bayesian estimates vis-à-vis various loss functions can differ considerably from often employed non-Bayesian estimates (e.g., ordinary least squares [OLS] limited information maximum likelihood [LIML], modified LIML, 2SLS, etc.), which are not optimal estimates in finite samples. However, since there is much interest in comparing Bayesian and non-Bayesian results, several non-Bayesian methods – namely OLS, 2SLS and feasible SUR estimates and forecasts – are computed. Of course, since the contemporaneous sector error terms are probably correlated, the SUR procedure may have an advantage over "single equation" methods such as OLS or 2SLS, especially if all the variables on the right side of the relation are predetermined and thus simultaneous equation complications are not present. Of course, if they are, then simultaneous equation systems methods, Bayesian, or non-Bayesian, can be employed that take account of error term correlations.

In forecasting experiments with eleven sector equations, annual data for 1952 to 1979 for the United States were employed to fit the sector equations. Then, using reduced form predictions of the two current aggregate variables appearing in each sector's equation, forecasts of each sector's real sales for 1980 were computed. These were then summed over the eleven sectors to obtain a forecast of real GDP and its growth rate for the US economy. Then, the sector estimates were updated using data for 1980 and the process repeated to get sector and aggregate forecasts for 1981 and following years through 1997. Such forecasts obtained from the sector forecasts were called "disaggregate forecasts." A main objective was to determine whether such disaggregate forecasts were better than forecasts obtained using just aggregate, annual data and several benchmark models.

Many have argued that disaggregation should be advantageous since with disaggregation the information in many more observations on the specific characteristics of sectors – e.g. agriculture, mining, construction, etc. – can be utilized to produce improved forecasts relative to forecasts derived from models using just aggregate data. Of course, if the sector models are not very good, it is not at all clear that disaggregation will improve forecasts. Indeed, in a published paper by Grunfeld and Griliches titled: "Is aggregation necessarily bad?" calculations are performed to support the contention that aggregation may result in improved results.[44] In my response, "On the Questionable Virtue of Aggregation," included in the appendix, I questioned the results of Grunfeld and Griliches' article. Indeed, there is unfortunately quite a limited literature on the analysis of the aggregation-disaggregation issue.

Note also that, with disaggregated data for eleven sector models, it is possible to use shrinkage forecasting techniques to make improvement relative to single sector forecasts. By adding the improved sector shrinkage forecasts, the forecast of the total is also usually improved, as shown in a recent paper.[45]

In what follows results of forecasting experiments will be reported that relate to the above issues after a discussion of the data employed in the forecasting experiments.

Data plots and forecasting results

A chart showing the eleven sectors' growth rates of real sales is shown in figure 1.6. As can be seen, the most volatile sectors are agriculture, construction, durables, and mining. This feature of the data is also apparent from the box plots presented in figure 1.7. In the future, it would be desirable to add variables to the analysis – e.g. weather variables, interest rates, inventory variables, exchange rates, world oil prices, etc. – to help improve the sector models. In the current experiments, "bare bones" sector models are being employed in an initial investigation as to whether it pays to disaggregate in terms of improving aggregate forecast performance.

In table 1.10 are shown the aggregate (A) and disaggregate (DA) models that are employed in the forecasting experiments. Benchmark aggregate models include an autoregression of order three, denoted by AR(3)(A), which has been widely employed. Another benchmark, aggregate model is the autoregressive' leading indicator model, AR(3)LI(A), an AR(3) model that includes the lagged rates of change of real stock prices and real money – leading indicator variables as shown in earlier empirical work. Finally, the third aggregate benchmark model that is employed is the ARLI model with added lagged level of real GDP and a time trend variable – an equation that flows from an aggregate version of the sector Marshallian model and thus is designated by MMM(A).

Also shown in table 1.10 are the aggregate reduced form equations for the real wage rate W_t, the first of which is an AR(3)(A) model, using the rates of change of W_t, namely $(1 - L) \log W_t$. The second aggregate equation is the same as the first with the addition of the leading indicator variables, the rates of change of real stock prices and real money, and is denoted by AR(3)LI(A). The final aggregate equation involves the addition of two lagged levels of the real wage and a time trend to the AR(3)LI(A) model and is designated MMM(A).

With respect to the sector DA forecasting equations, as shown in table 1.10, an autoregression of order three in terms of the rates of change of sector real sales, denoted by AR(3)(DA), is employed along with AR(3)LI(DA), Distrib.Lag(DA), and the other MMM(DA) disaggregated sector forecasting models, which differ with respect to how the level of real sales variables enter the relations. In the first model, denoted by MMM(DA)I, there is only one lagged level of real sales in the relation, while, in the next two models, real sales lagged two and three years enter and are denoted by MMM(DA)II and MMM(DA)III respectively. Finally, the last model incorporates the level of real sales lagged one year and the square of this variable in the model denoted by MMM(DA)IV.

In our forecasting experiments we compare the aggregate models' performance to that of the disaggregated models' performance in forecasting rates of change in aggregate US real GDP year by year, using RMSE and MAE as our measures of performance. Forecasting results for aggregate and disaggregated models are shown in table 1.11. Models were estimated using annual data for 1952 to 1979 and then used to forecast the real GDP growth rate for 1980 and subsequent years to 1997, with parameter estimates updated annually. For the aggregate models using aggregate data, least squares forecasts were used, while, for the disaggregated models and data, least squares and a number of alternative estimation and forecasting techniques were employed. The results show that it both pays to use the MMM and to disaggregate in forecasting annual rates of growth of real GDP for the United States. As summarized in our *Macroeconomic Dynamics* paper,

As regards the disaggregate forecasts shown in table 2B, it is seen that all of them have smaller RMSEs and MAEs than those for the aggregate and disaggregate AR(3) benchmark models. For example, the AR(3)(DA) model has RMSE = 2.26 and MAE = 1.65, whereas the disaggregate AR(3)LI, Distributed Lag and MMM(DA) models have RMSEs ranging from 1.40 to 1.98 and MAEs from 1.17 to 1.62 respectively. The lowest RMSE and MAE are encountered for the MMM(DA)III model fitted using the SUR approach, namely RMSE = 1.40 and MAE = 1.17. However, quite a few other MMM(DA) models had RMSEs in the 1.4–1.5 range and MAEs in the 1.2–1.4 range.

Thus, the results illustrate some benefits associated with disaggregation and use of the MMM's equations. In this connection, it should be recognized that several on-line forecasting units, including the US Council of Economic Advisors, the Wharton Newsletter and the University of Michigan, have had MAEs of forecasts in the vicinity of 1.2 percentage points for forecasts of annual rates of growth of real GNP in the period 1953–84, according to results summarized in the literature.[46]

Shown in figure 2.1 are plots of one-year-ahead forecasts associated with our models using "complete shrinkage" in fitting; that is, assuming that sectors' coefficient vectors are equal in value. It is seen that the AR(3) model missed all turning points whereas the other models performed better in this respect and in terms of RMSEs and MAEs of forecast, as mentioned above. Note from the plots that these models missed the 1990–91 downturn, when policy with respect to payments of interest on demand deposits changed. Use of a broader concept of money, e.g. M, rather than currency, in our models led to our forecasts catching the 1990–91 downturn; e.g., see figure 3B in the Zellner-Chen paper. In future work, at the suggestion of Milton Friedman, we shall also experiment with the M, money variable.

In summary, use of disaggregation and the Marshallian sector approach seems to be very promising not only in providing improved

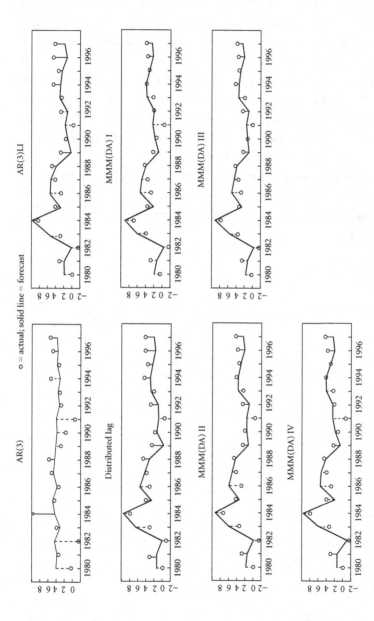

Figure 2.1 Plots of AR(3) and MMM forecasts and actuals

aggregate forecasts but also in providing sector forecasts that are of great interest to many. Further disaggregation by sector and region may also produce improved results of interest to many. Currently, we are working to close the model by adding factor markets for labor, capital, and money and government and foreign sectors in one, two and N sector versions of the model. Variants of the full model have been solved and used in experiments to study solution properties and impulse response functions' forms. When further results are obtained, it will be a pleasure to share them with you.

Thanks again to all for giving me the honor of presenting the first of the Sir Richard Stone Lectures, and best wishes for future success in this lecture series, which honors a truly outstanding person and scholar.

On the questionable virtue of aggregation

In a brilliant and provocative article entitled "Is aggregation necessarily bad?" Y. Grunfeld and Z. Griliches present some calculations
that they interpret as supporting the position that aggregation is *not*
necessarily bad.[1] As R. Solow points out, such a position runs counter
to "one of the deep-seated prejudices of the economics profession –
the belief in disaggregation."[2] But, even so, Solow – while calling for
more evidence and recognizing the intricacies of the problem – cites
the Grunfeld-Griliches paper approvingly.

Of course, the belief in disaggregation is more than a prejudice
on the part of the economics profession. As Orcutt and Rivlin state,
"That microeconomic data contain more information than the same
data aggregated is obvious. In general, one might expect some of this
extra information to be useful for purposes of testing and prediction."[3]
Further, the results of Theil on aggregation bias, even though limited
to *linear* aggregation (where one might think that the aggregation
problem would be least bothersome), cannot be anything but disturbing to those who rely solely on estimated macro-relationships.[4] In fact,
Grunfeld and Griliches (GG) devote a considerable portion of their
paper to an attempt to explain why it is that one of Theil's theorems
is contradicted by their empirical findings.

Given this extremely important issue of micro-versus macro-
analysis – one that has, among other things, vital implications for

the direction of economic research – it seems worthwhile to present an explanation of GG's empirical results, which apparently indicate that, in two instances, macro-relations have greater explanatory power than do the micro-relations underlying these macro-relations. Once set forth, the explanation will appear simple and obvious. That, in reality, this is not so is clear from the fact that many researchers who have analyzed micro-temporal cross-section data have failed to esti- mate their relationships in such a way as to utilize all the information in their data and thus to obtain the greatest possible explanatory and predictive power.[5]

GG analyzed two sets of data: one relating to investment demand and the other to fertilizer demand. Since the methodology and results were quite similar in both cases, we shall concentrate attention on just one of these analyses: that of investment demand. Annual data relating to each of eight corporations were first employed to estimate micro-investment functions. Then a "composite" measure of goodness of fit, R_c^2, was computed – a measure that GG constructed to show the percentage of the variation of the eight corporations' aggregate investment "explained" by the estimated micro-investment functions. This "composite" coefficient, R_c^2, was then compared with a squared multiple correlation coefficient, R^2, for a regression of the eight firms' aggregate investment on "independent" variables, each of which was a simple sum of corresponding explanatory micro-variables. It was found that the macro R^2 was slightly larger than the composite coefficient, R_c^2. GG interpret this result in the following words (1960, p. 3):

> The composite coefficient of multiple determination computed for the eight regressions is presented in the last row of table 1. It will be observed that this coefficient is *lower* than the coefficient of multiple determination of the aggregate regression. This result implies that, if we want to explain the *aggregate* investment behavior of the eight corporations, we are better off if we first aggregate all the variables

and then compute one regression than if we compute separate regressions for each firm and then "aggregate their explanations." If our aim were only to explain aggregate investment, we would have gained nothing from disaggregation.

To illustrate their approach as simply as possible, consider the case in which we have data relating to two firms. For these firms we posit the following micro-relations:

$$y_{1t} = \beta_1 x_{1t} + \alpha_1 + u_{1t}$$
$$y_{2t} = \beta_2 x_{2t} + \alpha_2 + u_{2t} \tag{1}$$

where the subscript t denotes period t, y_{1t} and y_{2t} are observed investment of firms 1 and 2 respectively, x_{1t} and x_{2t} are observed values of explanatory variables, u_{1t} and u_{2t} are disturbance terms and the α's and β's are micro-parameters. Now, in fitting the relationships in (1) by the OLS method, which GG utilized, we seek values of the α's and β's that minimize $\sum_{t=1}^{T} u_{1t}^2$ and $\sum_{t=1}^{T} u_{2t}^2$ or that minimize:

$$S_1 = \sum_{t=1}^{T} (u_{1t}^2 + u_{2t}^2) \tag{2}$$

For the macro-relation, derived from the micro-relations in (1), we have:

$$Y_t = \gamma_1 X_t + \gamma_0 + V_t \tag{3}$$

with $Y_t = y_{1t} + y_{2t}$, $X_t = x_{1t} + x_{2t}$, V_t a macro-disturbance, and γ_1 and γ_0 macro-parameters. In estimating equation (3) by least squares, values of γ_1 and γ_0 are sought which minimize:

$$S_2 = \sum_{t=1}^{T} V_t^2 \tag{4}$$

After having estimated the relations in (1) and (3), the following goodness of fit measures were considered:

$$R_a^2 = 1 - \frac{S_a^2}{S_y^2} \tag{5}$$

for the macro-relationship in (3) and:

$$R_c^2 = 1 - \frac{S_c^2}{S_y^2} \tag{6}$$

for the micro-relationships in (1). S_y^2, which appears in both (5) and (6), is the estimated variance of the macro-dependent variable in (3), S_a^2 is an estimate of the variance of V_t in (3), and S_c^2 is given by:

$$S_c^2 = \frac{1}{T'} \sum_{t=1}^{T} (\hat{u}_{1t} + \hat{u}_{2t})^2 \tag{7}$$

with $\hat{u}_{1t}$ and $\hat{u}_{2t}$ being computed residuals from the least squares estimates of the micro-relations in (1) and T' the sample size adjusted for loss of degrees of freedom due to estimation.[6] Since, as GG point out:

$$R_c^2 = 1 - \frac{S_c^2}{S_a^2}(1 - R_a^2) \tag{8}$$

the relative magnitude of R_c^2 and R_a^2 depends on the relative magnitude of S_a^2 and S_c^2.

It is important to realize that S_c^2 in (7) is based on $\sum_{t=1}^{T}(\hat{u}_{1t} + \hat{u}_{2t})^2$ but that the method of estimation employed to estimate the micro-relations minimizes the quantity S_1 shown in (2). On the other hand, S_c^2 is based on $\sum_{t=1}^{T} \hat{V}_t^2$, and this is just the minimal value of S_2 shown in (4). Thus, for the micro-approach, GG use one criterion to get estimates and a *different* criterion to construct R_c^2, whereas in the macro-approach the *same* criterion is employed in estimation and in constructing R_a^2. To obtain a similar consistency for the micro-approach as in the macro-approach, we should minimize:

$$S_3 = \sum_{t=1}^{T}(u_{1t} + u_{2t})^2 \tag{9}$$

rather than S_1, with respect to α_1, β_1, α_2 and β_2 to get coefficient estimates. That is, we minimize:

$$S_3 = \sum_{t=1}^{T}(y_{1t} - \beta_1 x_{1t} - \alpha_1 + y_{2t} - \beta_2 x_{2t} - \alpha_2)^2$$

$$= \sum_{t=1}^{T}[Y_t - (\beta_1 x_{1t} + \beta_2 x_{2t}) - (\alpha_1 + \alpha_2)]^2 \tag{10}$$

wherein Y_t is the macro-dependent variable.

Another way of rationalizing the minimization of S_3 to obtain estimates is to add the equations in (1) to obtain:

$$Y_t = y_{1t} + y_{2t} = \beta_1 x_{1t} + \beta_2 x_{2t} + \alpha_1 + \alpha_2 + u_{1t} + u_{2t} \tag{11}$$

and this gives the "explanation" of the macro-variable Y_t implied by the micro-system. Then minimization of S_3 is nothing more than OLS applied to (11).

Will minimization of S_3 to obtain micro-estimates change the verdict regarding macro- versus micro-goodness of fit? Fortunately, it is not necessary to do any computations to provide an answer. Note from (10) and/or (11) that the macro-approach involves minimization of S_3 subject to the constraint $\beta_1 = \beta_2$. Since a constrained minimum can never be smaller than an unconstrained minimum, we must have $S_3 \leq S_2$ with equality holding when $\beta_1 = \beta_2$. Thus, this micro-approach[7] will always do as well as, if not better than, a macro-approach in terms of goodness of fit.[8]

In summary, then, it can be said that GG's paradoxical results have been explained. When micro-data are analyzed in an appropriate fashion, it appears, *according to GG's criterion*, that these micro-analyses will be found not inferior to macro-analyses based on the same data.[9]

Notes

LECTURE 1: BANK OF ENGLAND

1. Deaton (1992).
2. Pearson (1938), Fisher (1956), Jeffreys (1973 and 1998), and Zellner (1980 and 1984).
3. Kuznets (1952). See also Friedman (1957) for additional consideration of Kuznets' findings.
4. Hadamard (1945).
5. Zellner (1984).
6. Quenouille (1957).
7. Zellner and Palm (1974).
8. McNees (1986), Fair (1992), Zarnowitz (1986), and Fisher and Whitley (2000).
9. Zellner, Kuezenkamp and McAleer (2001).
10. Bayes (1763). See also Dale (1991) for a lively discussion of Bayes' essay and various historical aspects of it, the volume edited by Geisser, Hodges, Press and Zellner (1990) on the relationship of Bayesian and Barnard's and others' likelihood approaches, and Goel and Zellner (1986) for material on Bruno de Finetti's Bayesian approach.
11. George and Nanopoulos (2001). See also Heckerman (2000) for materials relating to the Bayesian work of his Microsoft research unit, which was reported at the meeting but not included in the conference volume.
12. Zellner (1988, 1997a, 2002a and 2003).

13. See discussion following the paper by Zellner (1988) and in the Bayesian statistics text by Bernardo and Smith (1994). Also, the article by Barnard (1951), with discussion, and the text by Cover and Thomas (1991) provide some essential elements of information theory.

14. See Jeffreys (1998), pages 24–25, for a discussion of assumptions underlying the product rule of probability and his unsuccessful attempts to generalize them.

15. Dey, Ghosh and Strawderman (1999) and Zellner (1994) provide information about balanced loss functions and the properties of their associated optimal estimates and predictions.

16. See papers and references in Berry, Chaloner and Geweke (1996) and Zellner (1997a).

17. Diebold and Lamb (1997), Shen and Perloff (2001), Tsurumi (1990), Gao and Lahiri (1999), Park (1982) and Zellner (1997a, 1998) present results of Monte Carlo experiments comparing the sampling properties of Bayesian and non-Bayesian estimators using the widely employed Nerlove agricultural supply model and other simultaneous equations models.

18. See Stein (1956, 1960), Berger (1985), Jorion (1983, 1985), Min and Zellner (1993), Putnam and Quintana (1995), Quintana, Chopra and Putnam (1995), Quintana, Putnam and Wilford (1997), Zellner, Hong, and Min (1991) and Zellner and Vandaele (1975) for the theory and application of statistical shrinkage techniques in estimation, prediction and optimal portfolio formation.

19. Box and Tiao (1973), Leonard and Hsu (1999), Poirier (1991) and Zellner (1971).

20. The uniform prior was used by Laplace in analyzing this problem many years ago. Since then some alternative forms of priors for representing knowing little about the value of the binomial parameter have appeared and are discussed in the literature; see, e.g., Jeffreys (1998), Bernardo and Smith (1994), Leonard and Hsu (1999) and Zellner (1997a). As explained below, Bayesian posterior odds can be employed to appraise use of alternative proper priors and/or to combine results by averaging results provided by alternative priors. Also, in Zellner (1997b), it is shown how Laplace's problem can be solved in the Bayesian method of moments approach without employing a prior density.

21. For more on optimal estimates vis-à-vis alternative loss functions, see Berger (1985), Bernardo and Smith (1994), Berry, Chaloner and Geweke (1996), Leonard and Hsu (1999) and Zellner (1971, 1997a and 1998).

22. See, e.g., the Bayesian works cited in footnotes 19–21 and other Bayesian statistics and econometrics texts listed on the ISBA web page, www. Bayesian.org.

23. See my paper "Bayesian analysis of golf" (1999), presented at a research conference honoring George Judge, a fellow golfer, which can be downloaded from my home page: http://gsbwww.uchicago/fac/arnold.zellner. Also, as our dean Edward A. Snyder has pointed out, the analysis presented below can be applied to many other similar decision problems that arise in playing golf.

24. Leading definitions of probability are considered in chapter 7 of Jeffreys (1998). See also pages 30–33 for consideration of "utility-based" definitions of probability used by Bayes, Ramsey and others. It is indeed surprising that Jeffreys, a leading natural scientist, regards probability to be a measure of an individual's degree of confidence in a proposition – a subjective definition that he shows is very operational in applied scientific work.

25. Marsh and Zellner (1997).

26. Also, we obtained solutions in cases in which a target number of entering students and a target total expenditure level for student financial assistance are specified.

27. These references included work on problems relating to hotel room, airline seat and other selection or assignment problems.

28. See, e.g., Markowitz (1959). In later work, Markowitz (1987), he used Bayesian methods that were not available when he wrote his innovative 1959 book.

29. Bawa, Brown and Klein (1979), S. Brown (1976), Jorion (1983 and 1985), Quintana, Chopra and Putnam (1995), Quintana, Putnam and Wilford (1997) and Zellner and Chetty (1965).

30. Quintana, Chopra and Putnam (1995) and Quintana, Putnam and Wilford (1997).

31. For examples and references to the literature, see material and references in Berry, Chaloner and Geweke (1996) and Zellner (1971, 1984 and 1997a).

32. See references cited in note 31 for examples.

33. Zellner (1988, 1997a and 2002a).

34. Dempster (1968), Diaconis and Zabell (1986), Hill (1988, 1990), Just (2001) and references in note 33.

35. Fisher (1956). As regards Fisher's fiducial inference, which attempts to produce inverse inferences without introducing and using a prior density, see Jeffreys (1998, 381), who, among others, finds Fisher's argument defective.

36. Zellner and Min (1999).

37. Miller (1980).

38. Borch (1976).

39. Min and Zellner (1993).

40. See Min and Zellner (1993), where it was found that combining fixed and time-varying parameter time series models and their forecasts is possible and operational using posterior probabilities associated with alternative models and optimal combining predictive densities.

41. See, e.g., several papers in Berry, Chaloner and Geweke (1996) that have used Varian's asymmetric linex loss function in analyzing applied problems and provide references to the substantial literature on this topic. Varian's paper in which he introduced his linex loss function, "A Bayesian approach to real estate assessment," was published in Fienberg and Zellner, eds. (1975).

42. For an early collection of articles on Bayesian portfolio formation, see Bawa, Brown and Klein (1979) and Markowitz (1987). Recent work is described in articles by Quintana, Chopra and Putnam (1995) and Quintana, Putnam and Wilford (1997).

43. Brown (1976).

44. See Quintana, Chopra and Putnam (1995), Quintana, Putnam and Wilford (1997) and Jorion (1985).

45. Heckerman et al. (2000).

46. For further discussion and analysis see Berger (1985), Bernardo and Smith (1994), Press (1989) and other Bayesian texts.

47. For some work on the theory and application of the Bayesian method of moments, introduced in 1994, see Zellner (1997a and b), Zellner and Tobias (1999), LaFrance (1999), Tobias (1999), Soofi (2000),

Mittelhammer, Judge and Miller (2000) and van der Merwe, Pretorius, Hugo and Zellner (2001).

48. See references in note 47. See also Ryu (1990 and 1993) for innovative use of maximum entropy procedures in the analysis of various inference problems.
49. Golan, Judge and Miller (1996) and Mittelhammer, Judge and Miller (2000).
50. See, Zellner and Tobias (1999).
51. Good (1991). Also, Press and Tanur (2001) provide convincing evidence that leading scientists use much subjective information in their work.
52. See, e.g., some of the papers in Poirier (1991).
53. See Zellner and Vandaele (1975) for the prior that Stein used to produce his shrinkage estimate for his n means (1962, 266).
54. See Jeffreys (1998, 194), Heyde and Johnstone (1978) and Chen (1985).
55. Anderson and Rubin (1949).
56. Zellner (1983).
57. Diebold and Lamb (1997).
58. Nelson and Startz (1990), Zellner (1978, 1983, 1997a, 277ff.).
59. Tsurumi (1990), Gao and Lahiri (1999), Park (1982), Shen and Perloff (2001), Diebold and Lamb (1997) and Zellner (1998).
60. See, e.g., Dufour and Khalaf (2002) and references cited therein.
61. Soofi (2000). See also Soofi (1996) for additional useful, information theoretic results.
62. Hogarth and Einhorn (1992).
63. Fair (1992).
64. See Zellner and Palm (1974, 1975 and 2001).
65. McNees (1986) and Litterman (1986).
66. Fisher and Whitley (2000).
67. Zellner and Peck (1973).
68. Garcia-Ferrer, Highfield, Palm and Zellner (1987).
69. Burns and Mitchell (1946).
70. See Zellner, Hong and Gulati (1990), pages 390–393, for estimation results.
71. Hong (1989).
72. Wolff (1985).

73. Min and Zellner (1993). For earlier work on Bayesian variable selection procedures, see Zellner and Siow (1979).
74. Fildes (1994).
75. Wecker (1979) and Kling (1987).
76. Zellner (1958).
77. Zellner and Min (1999).
78. Hong (1989) and Min (1992).
79. Orcutt (1952 and 1957).
80. Zellner and Tobias (2000). See also Highfield (1986) for a procedure that may produce even better forecasting results for this disaggregated approach.
81. De Alba and Zellner (1991), Lütkepohl (1986) and Zellner (1962).
82. De Alba and Zellner (1991).
83. Veloce and Zellner (1985).
84. For plots of the output of such simple chaotic models as initial conditions and the parameter value are varied, see Kahn (1990, 428ff.) and Koop, Pesaran and Potter (1996, 124ff). In the latter reference, interesting generalizations of the basic chaotic model are considered.
85. Zellner and Chen (2001).
86. Zellner, Huang and Chau (1973).
87. Quintana, Chopra and Putnam (1995).

LECTURE 2: NATIONAL INSTITUTE OF ECONOMIC AND
SOCIAL RESEARCH

1. See Zellner and Chen (2001).
2. See Box and Jenkins (1976) and Quenouille (1957) for early work on time series analysis and Tinbergen (1937 and 1939) for pioneering work on econometric model construction and implementation.
3. Zellner and Palm (2000).
4. See Zellner and Palm (1975), reprinted in Zellner and Palm (2001).
5. Moore, Box, Kaitz, Pierce, Stephenson and Zellner (1981).
6. McNees (1986).
7. See Fisher and Whitley (2000).
8. Hamilton, Roberts, Pugh, Milliman, Goldstone and Zellner (1968).
9. Christ (1951 and 1975).

10. Nelson (1972) and Nelson and Plosser (1982).
11. Cooper (1972).
12. Adelman and Adelman (1959), Zellner and Peck (1973).
13. Fair (1992) and Zellner (1992).
14. Burns and Mitchell (1946).
15. Zellner, Huang and Chau (1973).
16. Huang and Zellner (1966).
17. Mittnik (1990).
18. Otter (1990).
19. Zellner and Min (1993), reprinted in Zellner (1997a).
20. Highfield (1992) and Tobias (2001).
21. Zellner and Vandaele (1975).
22. Swamy (1971), West, Harrison and Mignon (1985) and Kim and Nelson (1999).
23. Bates and Granger (1969). Also, Winkler (1981) provides one of the first, if not the first, formal Bayesian analysis of how to combine forecasts. For further Bayesian combining methods, see Zellner (1987) and Min and Zellner (1993).
24. Clemens (1989).
25. See, Palm and Zellner (1992) and Min and Zellner (1993).
26. Zellner (1987).
27. See Min and Zellner (1993).
28. Zellner and Hong (1991).
29. Zellner, Tobias and Ryu (1999).
30. Zellner and Min (1999).
31. Zellner and Tobias (1999).
32. Hong (1989).
33. Min (1992).
34. De Alba and Zellner (1991).
35. Lütkepohl (1986), Espasa (1994) and Espasa and Matea (1990).
36. See, e.g., some of the articles in Zellner (1997a).
37. See Veloce and Zellner (1985) and Zellner (2001).
38. See, e.g., Kahn (1990) and Koop, Pesaran and Potter (1996).
39. Zellner and Chen (2001).

40. These are discussed in various articles in Zellner (1997a) and in Dey, Ghosh and Strawderman (1999).

41. See, e.g., the summary of Monte Carlo experimental results in Zellner (1998).

42. For more on impressive, recent developments in computing techniques that have had a substantial impact on Bayesian analysis, see the articles by Geweke (1999) and Geweke and McCausland (2001) and the references that they cite. Also, in Berger (2000), references to free downloadable Bayesian software are provided, including the Cambridge BUGS and the Duke BATS programs.

43. Jeffreys (1998), Heyde and Johnstone (1978), Chen (1985).

44. Grunfeld and Griliches (1960).

45. Zellner (2002b).

46. See Zarnowitz (1986).

APPENDIX: ON THE QUESTIONABLE VIRTUE OF AGGREGATION

1. Grunfeld and Griliches (1960).

2. Solow (1960, 318).

3. Orcutt and Rivlin (1960, 321).

4. Theil (1954).

5. Compare Zellner (1961) and Zellner and Huang (1961).

6. It is not clear what GG used for T'. Further, it should be noted that taking $T' = T - k$, with k an integer, will not in general lead to an unbiased estimator of the variance of $u_{1t} + u_{2t}$ when u_{1t} and u_{2t} are correlated; cf. Zellner and Huang (1961), 14.

7. In some important senses this micro-approach is not the best one; Zellner (1961) cf. and Zellner and Huang (1961).

8. The argument is easily generalized to any number of micro-relations and any number of independent variables.

9. This statement in no way implies that macro-analyses should be abandoned nor that GG's criterion is an appropriate one. Perhaps a more appropriate criterion would be, say, a quadratic form in the forecast errors.

References

Adelman, I., and F. Adelman (1959), "The dynamic properties of the Klein-Goldberger model". *Econometrica*, 27, 569–625.

Anderson, T. W., and H. Rubin (1949), "Estimation of the parameters of a single equation in a complete system of stochastic equations," *Annals of Mathematical Statistics*, 20 (1), 46–63.

Barnard, G. A. (1951), "The theory of information," *Journal of the Royal Statistical Society*, Series B, 13, 46–59, with discussion by M. S. Bartlett, P. A. Moran, N. Wiener, D. Gabor, I. J. Good, F. J. Anscombe, R. L. Plackett and C. A. B. Smith, and the author's written response, 59–64.

—— (1997), personal communication.

Bates, J. M., and C. W. J. Granger (1969), "The combination of forecasts," *Operations Research Quarterly*, 20, 319–325.

Bawa, V. S., S. J. Brown and R. W. Klein, eds. (1979), *Estimation Risk and Optimal Portfolio Choice*, Amsterdam: North-Holland.

Bayes, T. (1763), "An essay toward solving a problem in the doctrine of chances," published in 1764 issue of the *Philosophical Transactions of the Royal Society, London*, 53, 370–418, and reproduced in S. J. Press (1989, 2003). [See the book by A. I. Dale (1991), cited below, for a detailed discussion of this paper with extensive references to the literature.]

Berger, J. O. (1985), *Statistical Decision Theory and Bayesian Analysis*, 2nd edn., New York: Springer-Verlag.

(2000), "Bayesian analysis: a look at today and thoughts of tomorrow," *Journal of the American Statistical Association*, 95, 1,269–1,276.

Bernardo, J. M., and A. F. M. Smith (1994), *Bayesian Theory*, New York: Wiley.

Berry, D. A., K. M. Chaloner and J. K. Geweke, eds. (1996), *Bayesian Analysis in Statistics and Econometrics: Essays in Honor of Arnold Zellner*, New York: Wiley.

Borch, K. (1976), "The monster in Loch Ness," paper presented at the CEDEP conference on foundations and applications of Bayesian methods, Fontainebleau 1976, published in A. Aykac and C. Brumat, eds. (1977), *New Developments in the Applications of Bayesian Methods*, Amsterdam: North-Holland, 273–278 (previously published in the *Journal of Risk and Insurance*, September, 1976).

Box, G. E. P., and G. M. Jenkins (1976), *Time Series Analysis, Forecasting and Control*, San Francisco: Holden-Day.

Box, G. E. P., and G. C. Tiao (1973), *Bayesian Inference in Statistical Analysis*, Reading, MA: Addison-Wesley.

Brown, S. J. (1976), "Optimal portfolio choice under uncertainty," Ph.D. thesis, Graduate School of Business, University of Chicago.

Burns, A. R., and W. C. Mitchell (1946), *Measuring Business Cycles*, New York: National Bureau of Economic Research.

Chen, C.-F. (1985), "On asymptotic normality of limiting density functions with Bayesian implications," *Journal of the Royal Statistical Society*, Series B, 47, 540–546.

Chib, S., and E. Greenberg (1996), "Markov chain Monte Carlo simulation methods in econometrics," *Econometric Theory*, 12, 409–431.

Christ, C. F. (1951), "A test of an econometric model for the United States, 1921–1947," in *Conference on Business Cycles*, New York: National Bureau of Economic Research, 35–107.

(1975), "Judging the performance of econometric models of the U.S. economy," *International Economic Review*, 16, 54–74.

Clemens, R. T. (1989), "Combining forecasts: a review and annotated bibliography," *International Journal of Forecasting*, 5, 559–583.

Cooper, R. (1972), "The predictive performance of quarterly econometric models of the United States," in B. Hickman, ed., *Econometric Models of Cyclical Behavior*, Vol. II, New York: Columbia University Press, 813–936.

Cover, T., and J. Thomas (1991), *Elements of Information Theory*, New York: Wiley.

Dale, A. I. (1991), *A History of Inverse Probability from Thomas Bayes to Karl Pearson*, New York: Springer-Verlag.

De Alba, E., and A. Zellner (1991), "Aggregation, disaggregation, predictive precision and modeling," working paper, H. G. B. Alexander Research Foundation, Graduate School of Business, University of Chicago.

Deaton, A. (1992), "Sir Richard Stone," proceedings of the British Academy, *Encyclopaedia of the Social Sciences*, 82, 475–492.

Dempster, A. P. (1968), "A generalization of Bayesian inference," *Journal of the Royal Statistical Society*, Series B, 30, 205–248.

Dey, D. K., M. Ghosh and W. E. Strawderman (1999), "On estimation with balanced loss functions," *Statistics & Probability Letters*, 45, 97–101.

Diaconis, P., and S. Zabell (1986), "Some alternatives to Bayes' rule," in B. Grofman and G. Owen, eds., *Proceedings of the Second University of California Irvine Conference on Political Economy*, Greenwich, CT: Jai Press, 25–38.

Diebold, F. X., and R. L. Lamb (1997), "Why are estimates of agricultural supply response so variable?" *Journal of Econometrics*, 76, 357–373.

Dufour, J. M., and L. Khalaf (2002), "Simulation-based finite and large sample tests in multivariate regressions," in R. J. Smith and H. P. Boswijk, eds., "Finite sample and asymptotic methods in econometrics," *Journal of Econometrics*, 111 (2), 303–322.

Espasa, A. (1994), "Comment on Zellner (1994)," *Journal of Forecasting*, 13, 234–235.

Espasa, A., and M. L. Matea (1990), "Underlying inflation in the Spanish economy: estimation and methodology," working paper, Bank of Spain.

Fair, R. C. (1992), "How might the debate be resolved?" in M. T. Belongia and M. R. Garfinkel, eds., *The Business Cycle: Theories and Evidence – Proceedings of the 16th Annual Economic Policy Conference of the Federal Reserve Bank of St Louis*, Boston/ Dordrecht: Kluwer Academic Publishers, 133–147.

Fienberg, S. E., and A. Zellner, eds. (1975), *Studies in Bayesian Econometrics and Statistics in Honor of Leonard J. Savage*, Amsterdam: North-Holland.

Fildes, R. (1994), "Research on forecasting," *International Journal of Forecasting*, 10, 161–164.

Fisher, P., and J. Whitley (2000), "Macroeconomic models at the Bank of England," in S. Holly and M. Weale, eds., *Econometric Modelling: Techniques and Applications*, The National Institute of Economic and Social Research, Cambridge: Cambridge University Press, 158–187.

Fisher, R. A. (1956), *Statistical Methods and Scientific Inference*, Edinburgh: Oliver & Boyd (2nd edn., 1959).

Friedman, M. (1957), *A Theory of the Consumption Function*, Princeton, NJ: Princeton University Press.

Gao, C., and K. Lahiri (1999), "A comparison of some recent Bayesian and non-Bayesian procedures for limited-information simultaneous equations models," paper presented to the American Statistical Association meeting, Baltimore 1999, Department of Economics, State University of New York at Albany.

Garcia-Ferrer, A., R. Highfield, F. Palm and A. Zellner (1987), "Macroeconomic forecasting using pooled international data," *Journal of Business and Economic Statistics*, 5, 53–67.

Geisser, S., J. S. Hodges, S. J. Press and A. Zellner, eds. (1990), *Bayesian and Likelihood Methods in Statistics and Econometrics: Essays in Honor of George A. Barnard*, Amsterdam: North-Holland.

George, E. I., and P. Nanopoulos, eds. (2001), "Bayesian methods with applications to science, policy and official statistics," papers presented to the International Society for Bayesian Analysis meeting, Crete 2000, Luxembourg: Office for Official Publications of the European Communities.

Geweke, J. (1999), "Using simulation methods for Bayesian econometric models: inference, development and communication," *Econometric Reviews*, 18, 1–126.

Geweke, J., and W. McCausland (2001), "Embedding Bayesian tools in mathematical software," in E. I. George and P. Nanopoulos, cited above, 165–173.

Golan, A., G. G. Judge and R. D. Miller (1996), *Maximum Entropy Econometrics: Robust Estimation with Limited Data*, New York: Wiley.

Goel, P. K., and A. Zellner, eds. (1986), *Bayesian Inference and Decision Techniques: Essays in Honor of Bruno de Finetti*, Amsterdam: North-Holland.

Good, I. J. (1991), "The Bayes/non-Bayes compromise: a review," president's invited paper presented to the American Statistical Association meeting, Georgia 1991.

Grunfeld, Y., and Z. Griliches (1960), "Is aggregation necessarily bad?" *Review of Economics and Statistics*, 42, 1–13.

Hamilton, H. R., E. Roberts, A. J. Pugh, J. Milliman, S. Goldstone and A. Zellner (1968), *Systems Simulation for Regional Analysis: An Application to River Basin Planning*, Cambridge, MA: MIT Press.

Hadamard, J. (1945), *The Psychology of Invention in the Field of Mathematics*, New York: Dover.

Heckerman, D. (2000), "Tutorials on learning Bayesian networks and papers online," www.research.microsoft.com/~heckerman

Heyde, C. C., and I. M. Johnstone (1978), "On asymptotic posterior normality for stochastic processes," *Journal of the Royal Statistical Society*, Series B, 41, 184–189.

Hill, B. M. (1988), "Comment on 'Optimal information processing and Bayes' theorem,'" *American Statistician*, 42 (4), 281–283.

(1990), "A theory of Bayesian data analysis," in S. Geisser, J. S. Hodges, S. J. Press and A. Zellner, eds., *Bayesian and Likelihood Methods in Statistics and Econometrics: Essays in Honor of George A. Barnard*, Amsterdam: North-Holland, 49–73.

Highfield, R. A. (1986), "Forecasting with Bayesian state space models," Ph.D. thesis, Graduate School of Business, University of Chicago.

(1992), "Forecasting similar time series with Bayesian pooling methods: application to forecasting European output," in P. K. Goel and N. S. Iyengar, eds., *Bayesian Analysis in Statistics and Econometrics*, New York: Springer, 303–322, with discussion and the author's response 323–326.

Hogarth, R., and H. Einhorn (1992), "Order effects in belief updating: the belief-adjustment model," *Cognitive Psychology*, 24, 1–55.

Holly, S., and M. Weale, eds. (2000), *Econometric Modelling: Techniques and Applications*, The National Institute of Economic and Social Research, Cambridge: Cambridge University Press.

Hong, C. (1989), "Forecasting real output growth rates and cyclical properties of models: a Bayesian approach," Ph.D. thesis, Department of Economics, University of Chicago.

Huang, D. S., and A. Zellner (1966), "The disaggregated short-run consumption function," paper presented to the Econometric Society meeting, Warsaw 1966, H. G. B. Alexander Research Foundation, Graduate School of Business, University of Chicago.

Jaynes, E. T. (1988), "Comment on 'Optimal information processing and Bayes' theorem,'" *American Statistician*, 42 (4), 280–281.

Jeffreys, H. (1973), *Scientific Inference*, Cambridge: Cambridge University Press (3rd edn.).

    (1998), *Theory of Probability*, London: Oxford University Press (3rd rev. edn.).

Jorion, P. (1983), "Portfolio analysis of international equity investments," Ph.D. thesis, Graduate School of Business, University of Chicago.

    (1985), "International portfolio diversification with estimation risk," *Journal of Business*, 58, 259–278.

Judge, C. S. (1987), "Problem isn't rate of U.S. savings, but where the money goes," *Wall Street Journal*, May 23, editorial page.

Just, D. R. (2001), "Learning and information," Ph.D. thesis, Department of Agricultural and Resource Economics, University of California at Berkeley.

Kahn, P. B. (1990), *Mathematical Methods for Scientists and Engineers*, New York: Wiley.

Kim, C.-R., and C. R. Nelson (1999), *State Space Models with Regime Shifting*, Cambridge, MA: MIT Press.

Kling, J. L. (1987), "Predicting the turning points of business and economic time series," *Journal of Business*, 60, 201–238.

Koop, G., M. H. Pesaran and S. M. Potter (1996), "Impulse response analysis in non-linear multivariate models," in S. Burgess, A. Escribano and G. Pfann, eds., "Asymmetries and non-linearities in dynamic economic models," *Journal of Econometrics*, 74 (1), 119–147.

Kuznets, S. (1952), "Proportion of capital formation to national product," *American Economic Review, Papers and Proceedings*, 42, 507–526.

LaFrance, J. (1999), "Inferring the nutrient content of food with prior information," *American Journal of Agricultural Economics*, 81, 728–734.

Leonard, T., and J. S. J. Hsu (1999), *Bayesian Methods: An Analysis for Statisticians and Interdisciplinary Researchers*, Cambridge: Cambridge University Press.

Litterman, R. L. (1986), "Forecasting with Bayesian vector autoregressions – five years of experience," *Journal of Business and Economic Statistics*, 4, 25–38.

Lütkepohl, H. (1986), "Comparisons of predictors for temporally and contemporaneously aggregated time series," *International Journal of Forecasting*, 2, 461–475.

Markowitz, H. (1959), *Portfolio Selection: Efficient Diversification of Investments*, New York: Wiley.

   (1987), *Mean-Variance Analysis in Portfolio Choice and Capital Markets*, Oxford: Basil Blackwell.

Marsh, L., and A. Zellner (1997), "Bayesian solutions to a class of selection problems," to appear in L. Marsh, ed., "Econometric analysis of higher education," *Journal of Econometrics*.

McNees, S. (1986), "Forecast accuracy of alternative techniques: a comparison of U.S. macroeconomic forecasts," *Journal of Business and Economic Statistics*, 4, 5–23.

Miller, R. (1980), "Actuarial applications of Bayesian statistics," in A. Zellner, ed., *Bayesian Analysis in Econometrics and Statistics: Essays in Honor of Harold Jeffreys*, Amsterdam: North-Holland, 197–212.

Min, C. (1992), "Economic analysis and forecasting of international growth rates using Bayesian techniques," Ph.D. thesis, Department of Economics, University of Chicago.

Min, C., and A. Zellner (1993), "Bayesian and non-Bayesian methods for combining models and forecasts with applications to forecasting international growth rates," *Journal of Econometrics*, 56, 89–118.

Mittelhammer, R. C., G. G. Judge and D. J. Miller (2000), *Econometric Foundations*, Cambridge: Cambridge University Press.

Mittnik, S. (1990), "Macroeconomic forecasting using pooled international data," *Journal of Business and Economic Statistics*, 8, 205–208.

Moore, G. H., G. E. P. Box, H. B. Kaitz, D. A. Pierce, J. A. Stephenson and A. Zellner (1981), *Seasonal Adjustment of the Monetary*

Aggregates – Report of the Committee of Experts on Seasonal Adjustment Techniques, Board of Governors of the Federal Reserve system, Washington, DC.

Muth, J. (1961), "Rational expectations and the theory of price movements," *Econometrica*, 29, 315–335.

Nelson, C. R. (1972), "The predictive performance of the FRB-MIT-PENN model of the US economy," *American Economic Review*, 62, 902–917.

Nelson, C. R., and C. I. Plosser (1982), "Trends and random walks in macroeconomic time series: some evidence and implications," *Journal of Monetary Economics*, 10, 139–162.

Nelson, C. R., and R. Startz (1990), "Some further results on the exact small sample properties of the instrumental variables estimator," *Econometrica*, 58, 967–976.

Orcutt, G. H. (1952), "Toward a partial redirection of econometrics," *Review of Economics and Statistics*, 34, 194–200.

  (1957), "A new type of socio-economic system," *Review of Economics and Statistics*, 39, 116–123.

Orcutt, G. H., and A. M. Rivlin (1960), "An economic and demographic model of the household sector: a progress report," in *Demographic and Economic Change in Developed Countries: A Conference of the Universities – National Bureau Committee for Economic Research*, Princeton: Princeton University Press, 287–318, and "Reply," 321–323.

Otter, P. W. (1990), "Canonical correlation in multivariate time series analysis with an application to one-year-ahead and multi-year-ahead macroeconomic forecasting," *Journal of Business and Economic Statistics*, 8, 453–457.

Palm, F. C., and A. Zellner (1992), "To combine or not to combine? Issues of combining forecasts," *Journal of Forecasting*, 11, 687–701.

Park, S. B. (1982), "Some sampling properties of minimum expected loss (MELO) estimators of structural coefficients," *Journal of Econometrics*, 18, 295–311.

Pearson, K. (1938), *The Grammar of Science*, London: Everyman's Library.

Pesaran, M. H., and G. C. Harcourt (2000), "The life and work of John Richard Nicholas Stone 1913–1991," *Economic Journal*, 110, 146–165.

Poirier, D., ed. (1991), "Bayesian empirical studies in economics and finance," *Journal of Econometrics*, 49, 1–304.

Press, S. J. (1989), *Bayesian Statistics*, New York: Wiley (2nd edn., 2003).

Press, S. J., and J. M. Tanur (2001), *The Subjectivity of Scientists and the Bayesian Approach*, New York: Wiley.

Putnam, B. H., and J. M. Quintana (1995), *The Evolution of Dynamic Bayesian Models: Applying Quantitative Discipline to Asset Allocation*, London: Global Investor, Euromoney Publications.

Quenouille, M. H. (1957), *Analysis of Multiple Time Series*, New York: Hafner Publishing Co.

Quintana, J. M., V. K. Chopra and B. H. Putnam (1995), "Global asset allocation: stretching returns by shrinking forecasts," paper presented to the International Society for Bayesian Analysis meeting, Istanbul 1995 (at www.Bayesian.org) and published in the joint ISBA and ASA section on Bayesian statistical science proceedings volume.

Quintana, J. M., B. H. Putnam and D. S. Wilford (1997), "Mutual and pension funds management: beating the markets using a global Bayesian investment strategy," *American Statistical Association's* (www.amstat.org) section on Bayesian statistical science proceedings volume.

Ryu, H. (1990), "Orthogonal basis and maximum entropy estimation of probability density and regression functions," Ph.D. thesis, Department of Economics, University of Chicago.

   (1993), "Maximum entropy estimation of probability density and regression functions," *Journal of Econometrics*, 56, 397–440.

Shen, E. Z., and J. Perloff (2001), "Maximum entropy and Bayesian approaches to the ratio problem," *Journal of Econometrics*, 104, 289–313.

Solow, R. (1960), "Comment," in *Demographic and Economic Change in Developed Countries: A Conference of the Universities – National Bureau Committee for Economic Research*, Princeton: Princeton University Press, 318–321.

Soofi, E. (1996), "Information theory and Bayesian statistics," in D. A. Berry, K. M. Chaloner and J. K. Geweke, eds., *Bayesian Analysis in Statistics and Econometrics: Essays in Honor of Arnold Zellner*, New York: Wiley, 179–189.

(2000), "Principal information theoretic approaches," *Journal of the American Statistical Association*, 95, 1,349–1,353.

Stein, C. (1956), "Inadmissibility of the usual estimator for the mean of a multivariate normal distribution," in *Proceedings of the Third Berkeley Symposium on Mathematical Statistics and Probability*, Vol. I, Berkeley: University of California Press, 197–206.

(1960), "Multiple regression," in I. Olkin, ed., *Contributions to Probability and Statistics in Honor of Harold Hotelling*, Stanford, CA: Stanford University Press.

(1962), "Confidence sets for the mean of a multivariate normal distribution," *Journal of the Royal Statistical Society*, Series B, 24, 265–296.

Stone, R. (1954), *The Measurement of Consumers' Expenditure and Behaviour in the United Kingdom, 1920–1938*, Cambridge: Cambridge University Press.

Swamy, P. A. V. B. (1971), *Statistical Inference in Random Coefficient Models*, Berlin: Springer-Verlag.

Theil, H. (1954), *Linear Aggregation of Economic Relations*, Amsterdam: North-Holland.

Tinbergen, J. (1937), *An Econometric Approach to Business Cycle Problems*, Paris: Herman et Cie.

(1939), *Statistical Testing of Business Cycle Theories*, two volumes, Geneva: League of Nations.

Tobias, J. (1999), "Three essays on Bayesian inference in econometrics with an application to estimating the returns to schooling quality," Ph.D. thesis, Department of Economics, University of Chicago.

(2001), "Forecasting output growth rates and median output growth rates: a hierarchical Bayesian approach," *Journal of Forecasting*, 20, 297–314.

Tsurumi, H. (1990), "Comparing Bayesian and non-Bayesian limited information estimators," in S. Geisser, J. S. Hodges, S. J. Press and A. Zellner, eds. (1990), *Bayesian and Likelihood Methods in Statistics and Econometrics: Essays in Honor of George A. Barnard*, Amsterdam: North-Holland, 179–207.

van der Merwe, A. J., A. L. Pretorius, J. Hugo and A. Zellner (2001), "Traditional Bayes and the Bayesian method of moments analysis for the mixed linear model with an application to animal breeding," *South African Statistical Journal*, 35, 19–68.

Veloce, W., and A. Zellner (1985), "Entry and empirical demand and supply analysis for competitive industries," *Journal of Econometrics*, 30, 459–471.

Wecker, W. E. (1979), "Predicting the turning points of a time series," *Journal of Business*, 52, 35–50.

West, M. P. J., P. J. Harrison and H. S. Mignon (1985), "Dynamic generalized linear models and Bayesian forecasting," *Journal of the American Statistical Association*, 80, 73–83.

Winkler, R. L. (1981), "Combining probability distributions from dependent information sources," *Management Science*, 27, 479–488.

Wolff, C. C. P. (1985), "Exchange rate models, parameter variation and innovations: a study of the forecasting performance of empirical models of exchange rate determination," Ph.D. thesis, Graduate School of Business, University of Chicago.

Zarnowitz, V. (1986), "The record and improvability of economic forecasting," *Economic Forecasts*, 3, 22–31.

Zellner, A. (1958), "A statistical analysis of provisional estimates of gross national product and its components," *Journal of the American Statistical Association*, 53, 54–65.

(*1961*), *An Efficient Method of Estimating Seemingly Unrelated Regressions and Tests for Aggregation Bias*, Report 6, 114, Econometric Institute, Netherlands School of Economics (published in the *Journal of the American Statistical Association*, 57, 348–168).

(1962), *On the Questionable Virtue of Aggregation*, Systems Formulation and Methodology Workshop Paper 6,202, Social Systems Research Institute, University of Wisconsin (reproduced in appendix of current volume).

(1971), *An Introduction to Bayesian Inference in Econometrics*, New York: Wiley (reprinted in Wiley Classics Library, 1996).

(1978), "Estimation of functions of population means and regression coefficients including structural coefficients: a minimum expected loss (MELO) approach," *Journal of Econometrics*, 8, 127–158.

ed. (1980), *Bayesian Analysis in Econometrics and Statistics: Essays in Honor of Harold Jeffreys*, Amsterdam: North-Holland.

(1983), "Canonical representation of linear structural econometric models, rank tests for identification and existence of estimators' moments," invited paper in S. Karlin, T. Amemyia and L. A. Goodman, eds., *Studies in Econometrics, Time Series and Multivariate Statistics in Honor of T. W. Anderson*, New York: Academic Press, 227–240.

(1984), *Basic Issues in Econometrics*, Chicago/London: University of Chicago Press.

(1987), "Bayesian and non-Bayesian methods for combining models and forecasts," working paper, H. G. B. Alexander Research Foundation, Graduate School of Business, University of Chicago.

(1988), "Optimal information processing and Bayes' theorem," *American Statistician*, 42 (4), 278–280, with discussion by

E.T. Jaynes, B. M. Hill, S. Kullback and J. Bernardo and the author's reply.

(1992), "Comment on Ray C. Fair's thoughts on 'How might the debate be resolved?'" in M. T. Belongia and M. R. Garfinkel, eds., *The Business Cycle: Theories and Evidence – Proceedings of the 16th Annual Economic Policy Conference of the Federal Reserve Bank of St. Louis,* Boston / Dordrecht: Kluwer Academic Publishers, 148–157.

(1997a), "Bayesian Analysis in Econometrics and Statistics: The Zellner Papers and View," invited contribution to M. Perlman and M. Blaug, eds., *Economists of the Twentieth Century* Series, Cheltenham (UK) Lyme (USA): Edward Elgar Publishing Ltd.

(1997b), "The Bayesian method of moments (BMOM): Theory and Applications," in T. Fomby and R. Hill, eds., *Advances in Econometrics,* Vol. XII, Greenwich, CT: Jai Press, 85–105.

(1998), "The finite sample properties of simultaneous equations' estimates and estimators: Bayesian and non-Bayesian approaches," invited paper presented to conference honoring Carl. Christ published in L. R. Klein, ed., *Journal of Econometrics,* 83, 185–212.

(2001), "The Marshallian macroeconomic model," in T. Nagishi, R. V. Ramachandran and K. Mino, eds., *Economic Theory, Dynamics and Markets: Essays in Honor of Ryuzo Sato,* Boston/ Dordrecht: Kluwer Academic Publishers, 19–29.

(2002a), "Information processing and Bayesian analysis," in A. Golan, ed., Information and Entropy Econometrics, *Journal of Econometrics,* 107, 41–50.

(2002b), "Bayesian shrinkage estimates and forecasts of individual and total or aggregate outcomes," paper presented to the American Statistical Association meeting, New York 2002.

(2003), "Some aspects of the history of Bayesian information processing," paper presented to the American Statistical Association meeting, San Francisco 2003.

Zellner, A., and B. Chen (2001), "Bayesian modeling of economies and data requirements," invited keynote address to International

Institute of Forecasters meeting, Lisbon 2000, published in *Macroeconomic Dynamics*, 5, 673–700.

Zellner, A., and V. K. Chetty (1965), "Prediction and decision problems in regression models from the Bayesian point of view," *Journal of the American Statistical Association*, 60, 608–616.

Zellner, A., and C. Hong (1991), "Bayesian methods for forecasting turning points in economic time series: sensitivity of forecasts to asymmetry of loss functions," in K. Lahiri and G. H. Moore, eds., *Leading Economic Indicators: New Approaches and Forecasting Records*, Cambridge: Cambridge University Press, 129–140.

Zellner, A., C. Hong and G. M. Gulati (1990), 'Turning points in economic time series, loss structures and Bayesian forecasting,' in S. Geisser, J. S. Hodges, S. J. Press and A. Zellner, eds., *Bayesian and Likelihood Methods in Statistics and Econometrics: Essays in Honor of George A. Barnard*, Amsterdam: North-Holland, 371–393.

Zellner, A., and D. S. Huang (1961), *Further Properties of Efficient Estimators for Seemingly Unrelated Regression Equations*, Systems Formulation and Methodology Workshop Paper 6,101, Social Systems Research Institute, University of Wisconsin, published in *International Economic Review* (1962), 300–313.

Zellner, A., C. Hong and C. Min (1991), "Forecasting turning points in international growth rates using Bayesian exponentially weighted autoregression, time-varying parameter and pooling techniques," *Journal of Econometrics*, 49, 275–304.

Zellner, A., D. S. Huang and L. C. Chau (1973), "Real balances and the demand for money: comment," *Journal of Political Economy*, 82 (2), 485–487.

Zellner, A., H. Kuezenkamp and M. McAleer, eds. (2001), *Simplicity, Inference and Modeling: Keeping It Sophisticatedly Simple*, Cambridge: Cambridge University Press.

Zellner, A., and C. Min (1993), "Bayesian analysis, model selection and prediction," in *Physics and Probability: Essays in Honor of*

Edwin T. Jaynes, Cambridge: Cambridge University Press, 195–206 (reprinted in Zellner, A. [1997a]).

(1999), "Forecasting turning points in countries' output growth rates: a response to Milton Friedman," *Journal of Econometrics*, 88, 203–206.

Zellner, A., and F. C. Palm (1974), "Time series analysis and simultaneous equation econometric models," *Journal of Econometrics*, 2, 17–54.

(1975), "Time series analysis of structural monetary models of the U.S. economy," *Sankya*, Series C, 37, 12–56.

(2000), "Correction to cointegration and dynamic simultaneous equations modeling by Cheng Hsiao," *Econometrica*, 68, 1,293.

eds. (2001), *The Structural Econometric Modeling, Time Series Analysis (SEMTSA) Approach*, Cambridge: Cambridge University Press.

Zellner, A., and S. Peck (1973), "Simulation experiments with a quarterly model of the U.S. economy," in A. Power and R. Williams, R., eds., *Econometric Studies of Macro and Monetary Relations*, 149–168. Amsterdam: North-Holland, 149–168 (reprinted in Zellner, A. [1984]).

Zellner, A., and A. Siow (1979), "Posterior odds ratios for selected regression hypotheses," in J. M. Bernardo, M. H. DeGroot, D. V. Lindley and A. F. M. Smith, eds., *Bayesian Statistics, Proceedings of the First International Meeting*, Valencia, Spain: Valencia University Press, 586–603.

Zellner, A., and J. Tobias (1999), "Further results on Bayesian method of moments analysis of the multiple regression model," *International Economic Review*, 42 (1), 121–140.

(2000), "A note on aggregation, disaggregation and forecasting performance," *Journal of Forecasting*, 19, 457–459.

Zellner, A., J. Tobias and H. Ryu (1999), "Bayesian method of moments analysis of time series models with an application to forecasting turning points in output growth rates," *Estadistica* (Journal of the

Inter-American Statistical Institute), 49–51, 3–63, with invited discussion and the authors' response.

Zellner, A., and W. A. Vandaele (1975), "Bayes-Stein estimators for k-means, regression and simultaneous equation models," in S. E. Fienberg and A. Zellner, eds., *Studies in Bayesian Econometrics and Statistics in Honor of Leonard J. Savage*, Amsterdam: North-Holland, 627–653.

Subject index

Author index

Printed in the United States
By Bookmasters